3·50

The story of
CLACK'S FARM

The story of
CLACK'S FARM

ARTHUR BILLITT

Ward Lock Limited · London

© Arthur Billitt and Riet Billitt 1981

First published in Great Britain in 1981
by Ward Lock Limited, 47 Marylebone Lane,
London W1M 6AX, a Pentos Company.

House editor Denis Ingram
Layout by Stonecastle Graphics

Text filmset in Hong Kong
by Asco Trade Typesetting Ltd.

Printed and bound in Hong Kong
by Everbest Printing Co. Ltd.

British Library Cataloguing in Publication Data

Billitt, Arthur
    The story of Clack's Farm.
    1. Clack's Farm (Hereford and Worcester).
    Gardens
    I. Title
    712'.6'0942440924   SB466.G73W7/

    ISBN 0-7063-5995-X

CONTENTS

To Riet, my wife, without whose help this book would not have been written

ACKNOWLEDGEMENTS

The publishers are especially grateful to Robert Challinor, who took all the black-and-white and colour photographs, except those on pp. 12, 25, 70, 74, 80, 92, 93, 118, 149 and 150. Robert Challinor's photographs were taken over a ten-month period and his ready co-operation to go to Clack's Farm at short notice on many occasions, in order to take advantage of suitable weather conditions, was much appreciated by both author and ourselves. We would also like to record that some shots—those taken from the roof of the Dutch barn and the main jacket picture—involved a measure of physical risk.

The publishers are also grateful to the British Broadcasting Corporation, Pebble Mill Road, Birmingham for providing details regarding photographic equipment shown in illustrations on pp. 25, 76, 85, 100 (lower) and 147.

The publishers gratefully acknowledge the following in granting permission to reproduce black-and-white photographs: British Broadcasting Corporation (pp. 93, 118 and 149), and James Fenemore Associates (p. 150). The publishers regret that they have been unable to identify the copyright holders of the photographs on pp. 12, 70, 74, 80 and 92, to whom acknowledgement is made.

All line drawings are by Nils Solberg. Fig. 5 is after the line drawing on p. 11 in *Percy Thrower's Guide to Gardeners' World*, BBC/Hamlyn, 1973.

Finally, the publishers would like to thank Geoffrey Smith for granting permission to quote the extract at the end of the description of the book on the dust jacket.

INTRODUCTION

Every story must have a beginning but seldom are the opening pages concerned with events fifty years ahead of the subject. For me the way to Clack's Farm was a very devious one, it started when at the age of six I invested my Saturday morning penny in a packet of pansy seed. At the time I was living in March, Cambridgeshire where my father operated several interests, a baking and corn merchant's business plus land for fruit and cereal growing. Close by the house was a stackyard where on a pile of unused bricks I placed a small wooden Cadbury's milk chocolate box and filled it with garden soil in preparation for sowing my pansy seeds. I remember being told to sow the seed evenly; my mother did the part that needed the extra care, covering the seeds with some sifted soil. When all this was done the box was covered with a sheet of glass, which amazingly survived in one piece in spite of the many times I deemed it necessary to have an inspection.

Success in germinating the seed posed another question: where were the seedlings to be planted? Looking back I shall always be grateful to my parents for the 3 × 3 m (10 × 10 ft) plot in their vegetable garden that my father dug and prepared for the reception of my very own pansy plants. This plot became my garden and as time went by I was given some 'Princess of Wales' violet roots which I propagated to make a complete border around the garden, and some border pinks. The purchase of a thornless rose 'Zéphirine Drouhin', which was far from being suitable for my little plot, completed my first garden and swallowed up my entire wealth of five shillings.

As the years went by my love for growing plants increased but according to my father that was not to be the way ahead for me. My two brothers, who were both more amenable to parental direction than myself, were—after leaving the March Grammar school—taken into the family business but I was apprenticed to pharmacy. After a three year apprenticeship which started at half a crown a week, I began to earn a little more and was able to save money. I had every intention to buy some land when I had saved enough and then if possible to start growing on my own account. Eventually I was able to fulfill my dream of having land of my own but starting from zero in the early thirties with a wife and child to support was not easy. It meant staying in pharmacy to pay the bills, whilst at the same time endeavouring to build up a horticultural business; it was a case of early to rise and late to bed. Appreciating my problems a generous local farmer and bulb grower gave me a wonderful start; he supplied the thousands of top quality bulbs, daffodils, iris, tulips and gladioli, each year at bare cost without expecting payment until after the flowers had been marketed and, what was even more vital, he was always at hand to guide and advise. By the time the Boots company purchased the two pharmacies in March I had gained enough experience and confidence in my ability to go it alone in horticulture. It was this confidence that enabled me to say 'no' to the suggestion that I should make pharmacy my career for life, but instead in a moment of enthusiasm put forward the suggestion that the Boots company should consider developing more extensively its business in the agricultural and horticultural field. This resulted in an invitation from the company to undertake a two-year investigation into how this could be achieved. At the same time I was asked to undertake some preliminary development and research work on possible new products for marketing in the agricultural and horticultural field. For the work I was promised the services of a chemist but the question of where I should be based for the two-year period was left to me. I decided that such a dramatic change in my career would necessitate leaving Cambridgeshire and giving up my own growing activities for the time being. It was a very hard decision to make and, but for the nationwide depression in 1933 and the low returns from commercially-grown flowers, there would now be no Clack's Farm story to tell. I would have stayed in the Isle of Ely to go on cultivating that wonderful fenland soil.

With the decision made I visited Kent and Worcestershire and decided that the answer lay in the vale of Evesham—with the Cotswolds farmland close at hand I felt that it was an area which could provide the facilities required. In September of that year we moved into a newly built house in Evesham and I started to make a new garden, an exercise which introduced me to some of the heaviest clay in the country and the two-tined fork. It was the first real test for my theory about the value of winter digging and it worked in practice, even after a wet winter the clay produced a workable soil and a good seed-bed in April the following year. Although I developed an affection for Worcestershire I still believed that one day I would go back to East Anglia and its kind fertile soil.

In September 1935 I moved to Nottingham, the Boots company's headquarters—as far as work was concerned this was a reward for efforts made and the opportunity to translate ideas into reality but it also meant living in or near a large city, which for me a country man was bound to be difficult. It was out of the question to go far out into the country as it was necessary to live within reasonable reach of good schools for my daughter Margaret. After the heavy clay of Evesham it was a relief to find that we could build a house just within the Northern boundary of the city on a plot of land where the soil was light and would be easy to work. However, I resolved then and there that on the day I retired I would go back to my native countryside.

The first four years in Nottingham with nothing more than a sub-urban garden to tend were relieved by the need to visit several hundred of the company's branches and to search for a suitable site for a research station. The quest for the latter was beset with many problems, the fact that I turned down the Beeston factory site, which at that time was subject to flooding, did not improve my relations with one of the senior directors. As the war clouds gathered in 1938 and again in 1939, Lord Trent, the chairman of the Boots company, stressed the need for positive action. Sometime during June 1939 I was invited to take tea with his lordship at Lenton House. After tea we walked into the garden and from there into a rough 1-hectare ($2\frac{1}{2}$-acre) paddock behind the house; here was the field that some years ago had accommodated the children's ponies. The subsequent period of neglect had produced thistles and nettles in abundance plus a good ground covering of couch-grass. For his lordship it had been for too long an eyesore. As we stood surveying the wilderness Lord Trent said 'Would this field be of any use?'. I replied cautiously, indicating that it might be, without mention-ing my thoughts about the possible use of the 13 hectares (33 acres) of parkland in front of the house. Lord Trent, never a man for delay, wanted my answer by coffee time the following morning. Armed with a spade I dug a couple of test holes, the soil was a heavy red clay, the type used for marling cricket pitches but the find of a land drain which had been working fairly recently tipped the balance. The next day at coffee time my answer was 'yes' and Lord Trent's reply was simply, will you please make a start. On that day the Lenton Research Station was born, to be followed later by the acquisition of the fruit research unit 15 miles away at Thurgarton.

With the almost immediate outbreak of World War II the 'Dig for victory' campaign became increasingly important and five demon-stration allotment plots were set up at the research station. During the wartime growing seasons, every Saturday and many weekday evenings

Lenton Experimental Station, subsequently known as The Lenton Research Station, Nottingham. The original potting shed cum office (photograph taken 1948).

Boots Horticultural Show, Nottingham, September 1944. C.H. Middleton (left) discusses marrows with the author and an official from the Ministry of Agriculture and Fisheries.

were given up to receiving parties of visitors for instruction on how to get the best results from small vegetable plots. After the war the emphasis at Lenton was directed entirely to research and a programme was agreed which included some of horticulture's outstanding problems. New laboratories, new greenhouses and special facilities were built, the scientific and practical staff was increased to tackle the testing and development of new compounds for pest, disease and weed control, at the same time work on plant nutrition and trace elements was undertaken. The fact that both the Lenton and Thurgarton ventures were proving to be successful, not only in producing new agricultural and horticultural products for the Boots company but also the knowledge that the quality of the crops grown was becoming a legend, made me feel that at long last I was beginning to satisfy my inward and deep desire to grow plants and not only that but even to grow crops well for research projects. However, being a planner by nature I began to think about the long term future, the time when I would retire and be no longer in charge of the Lenton Research Station, at the latest it would be 1967 so a plan for the future was essential.

My first task at that time, however, was to find a farm for my daughter Margaret who, after training at an agricultural college, was managing a poultry farm in Lincolnshire. I was anxious that Margaret should have the use of a property where she could develop her own pedigree poultry business. We agreed that Suffolk was to be the county, so in 1953 the search began. By this time my own ideas on where we might live postretirement had changed. I had been able to look at many of the English shires from an agricultural point of view and Herefordshire, not Cambridgeshire, was now going to be my definite choice for the future. So I was going to combine the two ideas and search for two places at the same time, aiming to get Margaret settled first.

Part I

FROM WILDERNESS TO NATIONAL SHOWPIECE

CHAPTER ONE

THE SEARCH AND THE DECISION

The search

As so often happens we found it relatively easy to define what we were going to look for but when we got down to the task we became more and more frustrated as the months slipped by. To start with Margaret's insistence on Suffolk limited the area of the search. We were agreed that a hundred acres would be about the right size for the pedigree poultry breeding venture. For me the purchase of a farm for poultry breeding could only be regarded as a long term investment; my faith in poultry farming in any of its forms was less optimistic than Margaret's, so in every instance other factors had to be considered. For me the quality of the land was going to be all important—I have always contended that houses and buildings can be altered and improved but that with land the basic qualities are unalterable, however hard one tries to effect improvements.

So with these guidelines in mind our almost weekly journeys started. We soon realised that the land in Suffolk was in the main either heavy clay or light poor sandy soil most of which was already in the hands of the Forestry Commission or planted with trees by private owners. Farms with better land in between these two types, with soils easy to work, higher fertility levels and good drainage, seldom came on to the open market. Sales of small farms with good land were usually transacted privately and we soon found that only properties with large acreages or small ones of doubtful farming value were widely advertised to stimulate the interest of unsuspecting outsiders. Our contacts with estate agents and auctioneers brought in a regular crop of glowing accounts of properties for sale; so many times did we set out from Nottingham full of hope only to discover that yet again the farm land was beset with problems which we were not prepared to take on board.

For over two years a spade in the boot of the car was a constant companion—on many an occasion a hole the depth of a spade in each field inspected told its own story about the soil and often to the surprise of the vendor we went on our way without even looking at the house or the farm buildings. I cannot resist suggesting that keen gardeners might sometimes follow our lead with advantage and take more note of the soil before purchasing a new or old property.

Having exhausted the possibilities and ourselves in Suffolk, we extended the search area to include the whole of East Anglia. However, it was all in vain. We met with no success at all, the sale of farm properties in Norfolk, Essex and Cambridgeshire following exactly the same pattern, only the dregs of the market being within our price range.

By the autumn of 1955 we were getting desperate, we all agreed that the search area should be further extended to cover virtually the whole of southern England and the Midlands. Margaret wrote to estate agents far and wide, arranging on one occasion for me to collect a pile of property particulars on my arrival back at Southampton Airport, following a visit to the Channel Islands, the idea being that I should visit some of the farms on my way back to Nottingham. This I did but again without finding anything akin to what we were looking for.

Amongst the papers were particulars of a property known as Clack's Farm, situated at Boreley, near Ombersley, Worcestershire. My first reaction was: too small, only 36 acres and in any case the name Clack's Farm was not on for a poultry farm with its clucking hens, so on to the back seat went the sale notice. It stayed there for weeks until March 1956 when I was in Worcestershire for two fruit growers 'brains trusts' meetings at Pershore and Ledbury. The night in between the two meetings was spent at the Lygon Arms, Broadway. After breakfast on the day of the Ledbury meeting, the Boots fieldsman for the area persuaded me to join him for some farm visits. This I was happy to do but by midday I was bored by his non-stop conversation and his somewhat moaning voice. Remembering that the Clack's Farm sale notice was still on the back seat I sought advice from Doug Harries, the then manager of the large Boots branch in Worcester. Doug gave me the full story, Ombersley was well known for its market gardening and black-and-white houses, and Boreley was not even a village, just a tithing close by the river Severn. Well, after five months the property would no doubt be sold but a look at it could provide a valid reason to escape from the chatterbox I still had as my companion for the day. When I arrived at the farm and found it was still unsold, I left my companion in the car on the side of the lane and ventured on to the property. The road was rutted, the old twisted iron farm gate and fencing had seen far better days, the corrugated iron roofs on the farm buildings were red with rust, the area near the buildings was scattered with old farm implements and equipment mostly covered by brambles and nettles. It was far too hazardous to attempt to establish just what else was lying around under cover. With this daunting outside picture I knocked on the back door and was duly ushered in through a dark narrow passage with its black-painted woodwork sticky with damp and lack of cleaning. In the dining-room I was offered a seat with a clear view of the door complete with its two rat holes and perforated zinc gauze ventilation panel. My chair rocked on the uneven quarry tile floor as the farmer and his wife unfolded their story; after a lifetime in farming they had bought Clack's Farm four years previously, then almost immediately ill health had intervened upsetting their plans. They were now being compelled to sell but after trying for more than two years on the market, an interested buyer was still not forthcoming. Remembering East Anglia, I came to the conclusion that here was a real problem farm, otherwise it would never have been allowed to go derelict in the first instance nor would the local farmers be so long disinterested in it, especially when it could be bought with its 14.5 hectares (36 acres) for £5500. Before leaving there was time for me to look at the soil if it could be found—weeds and rubbish were covering the ground in most places. The first spade holes revealed a reddish brown light to medium loam. Digging deeper I struck the old red sandstone; at last I was encouraged to go on. Here was property in a terrible state, with a local reputation it might not deserve.

The decision

It was that first handful of soil from the spade hole that called me back for a second visit, something I had never done previously in the whole of the two-year search. On this occasion I was not pressed for time, no chatterbox companion, even the owners were content to let me go it alone. So with the whole morning to spare I had a chance to walk around the farm alone; perhaps it would be more correct to say walk over the ground in some places and in others struggle around.

At the time the 14.5 hectares (36 acres) were divided into five fields, an old orchard, a small paddock near the entrance and a 2.5-hectare (6-acre) stretch of so called 'rough grazing' on a very steep, long bank which subsequently turned out to be a solid mass of bluebells in the spring followed by the most vigorous bracken. As I wandered around on this perfect spring day I was struck by the beauty of the surrounding Worcestershire countryside, arriving at the top of one of the fields I had a sudden first glimpse of the river Severn nestling in its green valley. On the opposite river bank were the Shrawley Woods and further beyond the Abberley Hills, all fully bathed in sunshine on this beautiful spring day. Here was England at its very best—any remaining desire to find a place in East Anglia evaporated instantly. I was almost in a trance of delight and happiness; I was seeing a small but special sample of heaven on earth in the English countryside. I turned round and looked back eastwards, there in the far distance was the farmhouse and the cluster of farm buildings, with a large field between me and the farm and none of the accumulated rubbish was visible. I was looking down from the highest point on the property and it was a view that aroused a vision. For the first time I saw possibilities—there in the distance could be a setting for a garden. I thought for a few moments then within me arose the determination to make that dream come true.

From the same view point I could see the remaining fields belonging to the farm, they were situated on the other side of a lane which bisects the farm into almost equal parts. The fact that on both sides of the farm the fields rose fairly steeply was clear enough. Even so this view did not caution me that Margaret's request was for flat fields in order that her poultry breeding units could be moved daily without too much effort. All the hedges were overgrown but these I knew could be brought under control given time. The junk, old farm implements, machinery and wire netting, the brambles, nettles, etc. could all be dealt with. What did still concern me was, why had this place got into such a mess, why had it been on the market for so long with apparently nobody prepared to buy it?

I collected random soil samples for analysis and a sample of water from the well, as without a safe water supply we could not consider purchasing any property. Before returning to Nottingham I surveyed the immediate area around the house. A search amongst the brambles revealed the remains of pighuts, feeding troughs, wire netting, etc. evidently undisturbed for years. Amongst all this rubbish hazelnut and holly seedlings had grown into sizeable trees. The boundary hedges, a glorious mixture of holly, thorn, brambles, ivy and traces of struggling box with tremendously thick basal trunks, were all over grown. The presence of the box in the hedges had a message, it told me that there once had been a garden here, much larger than the now small patch of rough grass in front of the house with its near dead pear tree and a few daffodils in straight rows, making a brave attempt to flower in spite of the competition from the couch grass.

With my interest aroused outside I looked over the house. It is not possible to describe all that I found but the sugar beet sacks on the kitchen floor and the ton of hay in the back bedroom, providing as it did a home from home environment for mice, gives some idea of the overall off-putting conditions inside.

As I travelled back home that afternoon I was hopeful but far from sure, there were so many questions still unanswered. The first answer came with a report from the Beeston factory laboratory that the water was 'pottable', in other words good drinking water. The report on the soil was not so good, it was very low in fertility and not to be recommended as a good buy, there were far better soils in the country more suitable for farming. A second set of soil samples were submitted, this time to a different laboratory but back came a similar report. In spite of these reports I still had an urge to go on and having agricultural contacts in the area I sought from them background information. It was then that the Clack's Farm story began to unfold; for over fifty years 'Old Charlie' and his stepson had lived in the house and farmed the land. Charlie was a character renowned for his home made cider and perry, it was he and his stepson who had left the farm machinery, etc. lying around where it had last been used. It was Charlie who had farmed the land to death growing potatoes and oats too frequently during the war years on the arable fields. Armed with this information I looked at a few self-set potato plants and some spring oat plants collected from a field where there seemed to be more mice than oats. An examination of both potato and oat plants in the laboratory gave the real answer: Clack's Farm's bad reputation over the past decade was due to potato eelworm and oat eelworm—for an arable farmer this would be really serious. Further detailed investigations showed that the eelworm problems were confined to three fields, the ones which Margaret intended to put down to grass and fold intensively with poultry. So in our case the trouble would not impose any immediate restrictions on the use of the land and I knew that grassing down and folding poultry over the land could well be a long term solution to the overall problem. In fact this has proved correct, we can now grow potatoes in a four-year rotation without a trace of eelworm appearing. With this further information it was time to invite the family to inspect the now possible property, Margaret and her partner Marie came over from Shouldham in Norfolk to Nottingham early one Sunday morning to join my wife and I for the journey to Worcestershire. On arrival at the farm Margaret's first comment was 'You said it was flat'. My wife was so shocked by the outside conditions that she fainted completely and was flat out before she even had seen the inside of the house. By pulling out all the stops I persuaded my wife that with determination the place could be made presentable and at the same time told Margaret that in addition to a horse she would need a tractor to move the poultry fold units—I promised to buy both straightaway. A tour of the house led to a general agreement that an immediate task would be some alterations in the house to make it fit to be lived in. In order to get an immediate decision I promised some alterations there and then which would enable me to press on with the purchase.

With this major hurdle dealt with the next stage was reached which included a farm valuation. The present owner had a forty-year Agricultural Mortgage Corporation loan of £4000 at 5% per annum, which our accountant insisted that we could not afford not to take on board. I did not agree but bowed to his financial expertise. After a complete tour of the land, buildings and house, the valuer took me in hand for a lecture on the risks involved in buying a derelict property such as Clack's Farm. His arguments failed to make any impression on me. I had made up my mind and that was it; at last I had found perhaps not what we set out to look for but land, buildings and a house with a challenge. I felt that even if the poultry venture did not succeed, Clack's Farm could be developed into something worthwhile. If it turned out to be nothing more than a garden in which we could grow plants for leisure plus vegetables and fruit to feed the family, I would be satisfied.

With very little encouragement, enthusiasm or support I pressed on in faith and with determination. A solicitor was instructed to make an offer of £5000 for the lot, finally it was agreed that we should purchase Clack's Farm at £5200 with the proviso that the giant, obsolete combine harvester with sprouting barley growing from all its crevices, should be removed by 30th July 1956, the day we were to take possession.

CHAPTER TWO

MOVING IN

Preparations to move in

Once the contract to purchase was signed we were committed; by this time Margaret had moved home from Shouldham in Norfolk to Stagsden near Bedford where Marie her close friend from their agricultural college days had taken a short term post. Marie then became the breadwinner for them looking after and rearing a vast number of turkeys, whilst Margaret was waiting and planning for the move to Worcestershire. Their stone-built Stagsden cottage was old and small, it could only accommodate a portion of their furniture, so for three months the rest was being stored in Nottingham. Starting a pedigree poultry breeding farm from zero is task enough when you are living on the spot but at a distance of 70 miles and the site in no way prepared for such a disciplined activity, the prospect was somewhat daunting.

Margaret's practical experience in her first post on a farm near Bury St. Edmunds then became invaluable. She decided to use their proven design for her breeding units, 1.80 × 1.20 m (6 × 4 ft) wooden houses on sleighs with 3.90 × 1.80 m (12 × 6 ft) tent like wood and wire netting covered runs. An order was placed for 20 units to be made by a firm in St. Ives, Huntingdonshire, for delivery the first week in August 1956. The nest boxes were to be fitted with special metal slide fronts that closed as the hens entered the nests to lay, a technique called trap nesting. Margaret choose two breeds—Rhode Island Reds and Light Sussex. With contacts in the specialist pedigree poultry world we purchased several rather expensive specially mated breeding pens of each breed, again for delivery in August.

Whilst all this activity was taking place on the poultry front, which at that time was the only reason for the purchase of Clack's Farm, I was building up ideas for a garden. I have always taken the view that a house set in a garden becomes a better home and at the same time provides an environment for really worthwhile living.

At Clack's Farm there was virtually no garden not even a record of there having been a garden. Poultry, even pedigree ones, however good looking and well bred, were going to be no substitute for plants. So I started planning too, a chat here and a chat there amongst horticultural friends soon brought offers of plants, shrubs and trees for when the site was cleared and had reached the planting stage. During the period May to July I called in at Clack's Farm several times to discuss small items, not included in the contract; these visits gave me the opportunity to look more closely at the area near the house. Here was just over a quarter of hectare ($\frac{3}{4}$ acre) according to the plans. The size I had to take as stated as it was too difficult to see as a whole in the wilderness of junk and uncontrolled growth.

At times the original vision seen from afar returned and I was still sure that with determination and endeavour a garden could be created. In any case time was going to be on my side—Rome was not built in a single day either. Then on other occasions when the sky was leaden and the rain was falling in large elongated drops, as it can in Worcestershire, the place looked so different, I needed Wellingtons and plenty of strength to pull them out of the quagmire after every step.

It was then that I decided to get George Reynolds, the Lenton Research Station foreman, to have a look at the proposed site for the garden. George, as honest as the day is long, always found it difficult to hide his thoughts and I knew that I could rely on his down to earth opinion. Before we got to the farm he asked how we had ever found the place in the first instance, the two miles of narrow lanes from the main road evidently did not meet with his approval. His face dropped dramatically as we entered the farm gate; at that moment he was speechless. We started to walk round and got to the point where it was just possible to peer into the potential garden area, George kept silent and listened intently whilst I unfolded my ideas; it was his candid opinion I wanted. George had spent a lifetime gardening and had designed and made many gardens before he joined the Boots Company at the Lenton Research Station. He looked absolutely bewildered and remained silent, then I posed the question: 'What do you think of it George?'. I shall never forget his reply: 'You will need a heart as large as a frying pan to tackle it'. There have been many times since when I have felt that George was right in his assessment of the task. So even George had joined the rest in voicing an opinion which gave me little encouragement.

I had sometimes nervously realised that it was going to be a challenge making a garden whilst the rest of the family were more interested in making the poultry side of the business a success. By this time I was completely resigned to the fact that creating a garden at Clack's Farm was going to be a formidable task, especially as I was determined to do the job myself or not at all. It was now a question of making arrangements for the two lots of furniture to arrive at Clack's Farm at midday on 30th July and wait for that eventful day.

If only I had known at the time that I stood on the high point and viewed the countryside with the farm in the far distance, that this particular field in 1873 was called Mount Pleasant, I would have felt at least that someone else in the past had had a similar vision. On second thoughts maybe another field across the lane called Clay Pitts might well have put me off, so perhaps it is just as well that I looked at Clack's Farm as it was rather than the 1873 layout plan of the fields.

The move in: 30th July 1956

Up till now all my thoughts and plans for the future had been solely concerned with the land and how we would deal with it and its problems. Now with our two furniture vans arriving at precisely the same time as the farmer and his wife (together with their belongings) were departing, I realised that the house and its problems were going to be on the immediate agenda. From past experience I know that no house looks its best without furniture, pictures, curtains and carpets, but from the moment I stepped inside this one it appeared scarcely habitable. On entering the house the long narrow passage from front to back door was dark, not a trace of daylight could enter it to light the way. Halfway along the passage was a black, farm-building-type door behind which were brick steps down to the cellar. Here it was dark and damp and its musty smell pervaded the whole house. The dining-room greeted us with its uneven quarry tiles laid directly on the soil, its ingle-nook fireplace completely spoiled by a home-made brick fireplace in the centre. The overmantle and side panels were made of pitch pine but vandalized and ruined by having been either tarred or given several coats of black paint, which was now sticky with damp and dirt.

Leading off the dining-room was a so-called farm office; it was damp beyond imagination, the wall paper hung adrift from the walls, the plaster had crumbled away and most of it was now on the floor. The kitchen walls were covered with large sheets of asbestos, some were cracked where the holding screws were too tight, the floor was covered with old sugar-beet sacks underneath which was hardpacked damp soil.

Across the passage was the scullery with its oak beams and giant metal hooks, where no doubt the sides of bacon and ham had hung in more prosperous days. In one corner of the scullery was a coal-fired bread oven, in the other corner was a brick built copper, all indicating that this

BBC2 'Gardeners' World' cameraman, prepares to shoot, while the author awaits the cue for action. Note the cameraman's headset and microphone, which enable him to communicate with the producer. In the far background is Mount Pleasant which overlooks the river Severn (September 1973).

The house, prior to the extension, with its original front door, facing south. The ornamental garden begins to take shape — note the young *Prunus avium* 'Plena' (ornamental cherry) recently planted in the lawn (July 1964).

South-west aspect of house and lawn in autumn 1979 (upper) and winter 1979 (lower). On the left is a *Betula pendula* 'Youngii', on the right (overhanging) a flowering cherry 'Yukon'.

South-east aspect of house and lawn in spring 1980 (upper) and summer 1980 (lower).
Note the now mature *Prunus avium* 'Plena'.

Left: Our stone lady, of great age, with an unrecorded history, mounted on a straddle stone and clothed in ivy, and situated at the west end of the ornamental garden.

Below: One of the dozen straddle stones at Clack's Farm, this one as seen from the kitchen window. In the background is the 16th century black-and-white farm worker's cottage (spring 1980).

was the oldest part of the house and probably dating back to the 16th century as did the cellar with its hand-hewn, sandstone walls. The low sink in the scullery had been shaped out of a solid block of Forest of Dean stone. It bore signs of centuries of wear—there was still the hole at one end where at one time the pump had stood. As everywhere else downstairs the floor was damp and uneven, the red quarry tiles were worn and broken; they told the story of the days before Wellingtons when farmers' boots had solid hobnailed soles.

Next to the scullery door a narrow back staircase led up into a bedroom which was almost filled with old hay, a home from home for quite a number of mice. It was not until a few days later when we started to clear the hay out that we discovered some other very unwelcome life around. I started to itch and the trouble got worse, so at last when scratching did not ease matters I decided to investigate more closely—to my horror I was almost covered in red spots. I stripped outside leaving every piece of clothing where it fell. After a bath in almost cold water the itching subsided and I was ready to treat the remaining hay with DDT dust. A day or two later I plucked up courage to try again; it was then just old hay, the DDT had done its job.

The main staircase started from close by the front door—it was narrow, spiral and almost vertical and had been made by craftsmen of long ago, who had chosen the finest pitch pine wood I have ever seen. A few years later it was condemned to go—Margaret slithered from top to bottom several times and the rest of us only survived by clutching strongly to the handrail as we ventured either up or down. The other three bedrooms were reasonable; the single-sash windows were small as in the rest of the house but from the two bedrooms at the front we could see the Malvern Hills, about 15 miles away in the distance.

Prospecting the outside of the house I came to the conclusion that many a decade had gone by since the window frames had been painted; most of the putty had crumbled away, each pane of glass being held in by only two or three small nails. The front of the house faces due south and when I came to the west side I discovered a vine, uncared for but still struggling to produce a few bunches of small berries. It turned out to be a 'Black Hamburg' and it survived until the final reconstruction and extension work in 1966. A couple of steps from the vine was the outside toilet complex housed in a brick building attached to the house wall. From the inside layout we concluded that at some time or other a large family had lived here. The whitewood benching had three separate openings, each fitted with a wooden lid, sized appropriately for father, mother and child. Underneath the seating the ashpit was very off putting and it was months before I had the courage and the strength of mind to deal with it. Like the vine the outside toilet disappeared in 1966.

We straightway decided to employ a local builder, who dealt with the floors and removed the bread oven and brick copper. In their place we put in a toilet complete with water flushing at the bidding of a handle— the wind of change had started to blow at Clack's Farm.

To help in the moving operation I had taken a fortnight's holiday, the first week was hectic both in the house and outside. The poultry breeding pen units were delivered and the hens and cockerels arrived soon afterwards. As a result there was not much time for regular meals or in fact for the preparation of food generally. We soon found that the small black plums on a long row of trees were just about ripe, although the skins seemed unusally tough. Well, being fond of plums and custard, a quick and easy dish to prepare, I almost lived on it. By the beginning of the second week I was laid low with a dreadful pain, sufficiently bad to make the decision to go back to Nottingham where my doctor ordered me straightway into hospital. After some investigations, including an X-ray, all they could find was that an excess of Clack's Farm plum skins had set up the trouble. The plum trees were soon pulled out and since then I have had no further trouble.

Local reaction

There must always be a risk of resentment when an outsider ventures to acquire a farm property, especially if it is in a deep countryside area where the local community is a tightly knit one. The tithing of Boreley, with its dozen or so inhabitants and having no new houses built there since before the first world war, is just that, and could well have been upset by our intrusion. In fact the reverse was true. Here I give credit to Margaret for her diplomacy, from the first day onwards it was such that before the end of the first week Bert Gregg a member of a well-known local family walked in and made himself known. Bert told me that he had known Clack's Farm from childhood—his stories about 'Old Charlie' could fill another book. I am convinced that Bert felt terribly sorry for us all, having saddled ourselves (according to him) with a problem for life—doubtless we needed help without the cost of employing labour otherwise we, too, might go broke. Now, after 25 years, Bert still comes in when he feels like it, and that is fairly often—he trims the hedges, mows the lawns and is always more than willing to have a go at any job, however heavy it may be.

Bert is a happy man, he lives with his brother Peter and sister Ethel in a black-and-white cottage close by the Severn; his way to Clack's Farm is up an unmade lane alongside our bluebell and bracken bank. For

Bert Gregg, always happy to lend a hand at Clack's Farm, cutting up a large fruiting cherry tree, which sadly died of old age.

the inward journey the lane is too steep for cycling but Bert brings his bike to Clack's Farm so that he can free-wheel home for lunch or tea. In these materialistic days our visitors find it difficult to believe our story about Bert who helps us all the year round without payment. For Bert his reward is far more valuable, he knows that for a quarter of a century he has made a considerable contribution towards making Clack's Farm what it is today, an environment for happy and satisfactory living both for Bert and ourselves. We are always pleased to see Bert, even if it is only for a coffee and a piece of cake. We enjoy his stories about the old days of Clack's Farm and 'Old Charlie', the times when very potent cider and perry were made here, the brews apparently always being on the strong side. Bert is also the person who keeps us up to date about what is happening around us; it is he who often reports the arrival of the cuckoo in Shrawley Wood across the river. As a keen observer it is usually Bert who spots the first nightingale in the trees before it starts its lovely song during the warmer weather in May when it starts to lay its eggs.

Having spent my life up to that time in areas beyond the range of the nightingale and in places where the yellow wagtails deemed not to live, I decided at this early stage that the $2\frac{1}{2}$ hectares (6 acres) of so-called rough grazing should be left and kept as a nature reserve. To this day it is still untouched and in spite of having lost some of the old trees we still see from time to time the green woodpecker and its relatives, the lesser and greater spotted woodpecker. The pleasure they give us and our visitors is beyond price. Bert was right in suggesting that we kept it as it was, with the proviso that we should take great care each autumn when the bracken would be tinder dry. In the 25 years it has only been on fire once, deliberately set alight in the lane by a youth. It was very frightening and Marie, with her clothes alight was very near to losing her life; it was Margaret's quick action that prevented a tragedy.

'Click' Moss was a real local character who loved giving us advice, he suggested that we should put pigs on the bank—they would root up the bracken and bluebells, he said, and we would make some money in the bargain. Whilst we did not take Click Moss's advice to keep pigs, his wish to put a half dozen young cattle in Sawpit piece seemed fair enough. It was a square, three-acre field with plenty of grass; the hedges were overgrown but the strands of old barbed wire that had been in them for years would keep the cattle from getting out. I knew that grazing the grass would be good for the land. Click was short of 'keep' and wished to put them out to 'tack'. 'Well mister,' he asked 'would a pound a week be alright?'. We agreed and from then on every Sunday morning he turned up sucking his old pipe, with more than a little juice dropping on his well-worn coat. How I wish I had taken a photograph of this country character of a past age fumbling in his tattered tobacco pouch for an equally tattered pound note. Although extremely crumpled and dirty, the notes were accepted if only for their aromatic odour— I am still not sure whether Click smoked tobacco or dried leaves from the hedgerows. Click was very concerned when we started to plant some flowering cherries in the fields alongside the lane, 'They won't make any money for you mister,' he said. 'Well, supposing I have some money, what then?' I answered. His answer to that was 'If you be in that fortunate position you can please yourself mister' and that is what I did.

Other locals were more forthright, one told me quite bluntly that I must have been a fool to buy Clack's Farm—it never had been any good and never would be any good, that was why he and others had not touched it when it came on the market. Buying it was bad enough but when they saw me planting ornamental cherries in full view of everyone using the lane, it was suggested that this chap at Clack's Farm might be inside 'ere long. Surely he must be mad to be doing such ridiculous things; he will go broke like the rest of them, before long.

Another person did not think me so mad to have bought the place; he came on the second Sunday morning in an attempt to put us off living in the house. Here 'Old Charlie', according to him, had behaved far below acceptable standards, the dining-room, for instance, had been more comfortable than the outside toilet. On top of that 'Old Charlie's' ghost haunted the place and we could expect another ghost; Old Charlie's stepson had committed suicide on the premises. Having done his utmost to either frighten us or turn us against Clack's Farm for ever, he made an offer to buy the place. In spite of my firm reply he continued to make a case, his stories got more lurid as he went on—finally we got rid of him.

It was fortunate that neither Margaret nor Marie are upset by ghosts having had the experience of one who walked the fields in Suffolk, always dressed in white on still evenings and another one in Stagsden who appeared in a black shroud. As for me, I would not recognise one if I saw one and in any case a trifle such as a ghost was not going to put me off the place.

It was a year or two later that a lady walked in to tell me that I would never make a garden the way I was going about it. She certainly did not approve of the way I was planting trees whilst the area still looked like a junk yard. What she did not see were the circles of cleared ground amidst the rubbish; it was in these circles that I was planting. I tried to tell her that trees took longer to grow than shrubs or other plants but she would not listen. I had started with a mental picture of a garden with trees as a backcloth and this would be planted first, whether the good lady approved or not.

The largest farmer in the district was not too pleased with the Billitts; he was farming land next door. Whilst Clack's Farm was sticking on the market for so long without a buyer he could wait and in due time hope to buy the property at his price, as he had done in the district so often before. The factor that prevented this happening was apparently the lack of love between the would-be purchaser and the seller. This was fortunate for us otherwise there would be no Clack's Farm story to tell.

My dislike of the name Clack's was such that by the time we moved in we had a stock of headed writing paper ready with the farm's new name on it: 'Cherry Hill Farm'. We used the writing paper with great pride but alas no replies reached us by post. Then the reason filtered through; letters addressed to us were being returned 'Unknown'. One Saturday morning I met up with the old postman in a nearby lane and asked why these letters should have been returned, as they were clearly addressed to Cherry Hill Farm. His reply was positive in the extreme: 'There ain't such a place here'. I pointed to the farm in the distance. 'That be Clack's farm, it always has been and always will be', came the reply. His ruling was final; if we wanted letters they would have to be addressed correctly, otherwise back they would go. So the new writing paper became scrap and we were going to have to live with the name Clack's Farm for ever and a day. On reflection the old postman was right; down through the centuries from Elizabethan times it had always been Clack's. According to some the name relates to its use as a watering place for cattle on the move and this may well be right as our well had never been known to run dry. Before attempting to alter the name we would have been wise not only to consult the old postman but also the ordnance survey map on which it is clearly marked. Now we realise the value of such an unusual name—there are many Cherry Hill Farms but only one Clack's Farm and we do still post some of our letters in a wall letter box with E.R. VII embossed on it, so even the post office does not change for change's sake in our part of the Worcestershire countryside.

CHAPTER THREE

THE HOUSE

Looking back at the property

The deeds of Clack's Farm go back to 1873 when a Mr. John Tracey Wood of the parish of Claines, Worcester sold Clack's Farm to a Dr. Serjeant Samuel Roden of Droitwich for £3235, who started off with a mortgage of £1673.8.6 Two years later he took up a second mortgage of £902.5.0. By 1879 the Roden trust was set up when Dr. Roden together with John Grazebrooke Wood, Ann Glasbrooke and John Harris borrowed another £900.

After a few years this was followed by another £2700, with some other properties in Droitwich involved. In 1897 the Roden Trust sold Clack's Farm for £1200 and it was then that Charles Hodges of Kidderminster became the owner. 'Old Charlie' as he was later known locally remained in possession until his death in 1953, although during the 56 years of 'Old Charlie's' reign there were periods of change. In 1916 he sold Clack's Farm for £1400 but stayed on as tenant; in 1919 he bought it back for £2000, having to borrow £1000 to do so. After 'Old Charlie's' death in 1953 and his stepson's death by his own hand soon afterwards, there was a farm sale of implements and the property itself was sold for £4750.

The new owner started with intentions to make improvements both inside and out—whether all of them were wise I would doubt. By farming standards 14.5 hectares (36 acres) is a small unit; the expense of building a new four-bay Dutch barn must have been considerable, as was the installation of piped water into the house together with the very long runs of copper piping to cattle troughs in two fields.

After 25 years, the electric pump the new owner installed $13\frac{1}{2}$ m (45 ft) down in the old red sandstone bore still works efficiently at the call of a ball and valve in the roof space tank. We are more than grateful for the constant supply of the near-Malvern quality water, free from chlorine. It is ideal for watering the most tender plants and it makes a superb cup

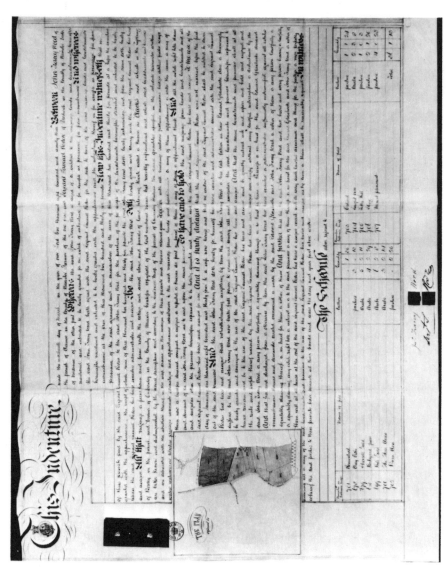

Photographic reproduction
of the original Deeds of
Clack's Farm, dated
19 March 1873.

of tea, so all our visitors claim. Another costly improvement undertaken by him was the introduction of electricity, although the house wiring was all on the surface; outside lighting points were put into every building. Inside, the kitchen walls were clad with asbestos sheeting, and the small bedroom converted into a bathroom. These expenditures on nonproductive improvements, quickly followed by an illness which ruled out his farming activities, was an unfortunate happening which produced financial problems and the situation where we came in to buy the property.

Going back to 1873, when the property was known as 'Clack's', the boundaries were identical to those of today, although the fields were smaller, eleven in all, eight on the house side of the lane and three on the other side. Looking at the list of fields (see the Deeds' photograph and Fig. 1), each with its number and name is quite fascinating. Starting across the lane with Clay Pitts, Sherrell Field and Rickyard Piece, which clearly reveals that clay was worked here and contrary to general belief there is still clay here in the make-up of the soil. Coming across the lane, near the front gate was Barn Close, then Sawpit Piece going down to Little Hill and along the bottom lane runs the Sling, now our bluebell and bracken covered nature reserve.

Orchard, now the TV fruit and vegetable garden, is adjacent to the rising ground which was called The Three Acres and over the rise is Hill Field, which looks down to the Severn and its water meadows. The corner where Sling and Hill Field meet has a delightful name, Mount Pleasant—it's the spot from which I got my first view of the Severn valley and the local Worcestershire countryside, which fortunately is still unspoilt. This leaves until last Homestead, the area where the house stands, which in 1873 apparently had a surrounding garden of approximately $\frac{1}{4}$ hectare ($\frac{3}{4}$ acre), no doubt more utilitarian than our present ornamental garden.

By 1956, the time we bought Clack's Farm, Little Hill, Sling and Mount Pleasant had been brought together to form 3.1 hectares (7.7 acres) of so called rough grazing. Three Acres and Hill Field had also been merged into one arable field—it was free of crops but smothered with weeds, both annuals and perennials. The ground underneath was reasonably level so could be left to 'tumble down', an old fashioned method for establishing grass without the cost of seeding. With the new Ferguson tractor and Hayter rotary mower we planned to master the weeds sufficiently to allow the indigenous grasses to take over, it would then be up to the poultry to naturally replenish the fertility, which they did thoroughly, manuring each area before being moved on at the beginning of each day.

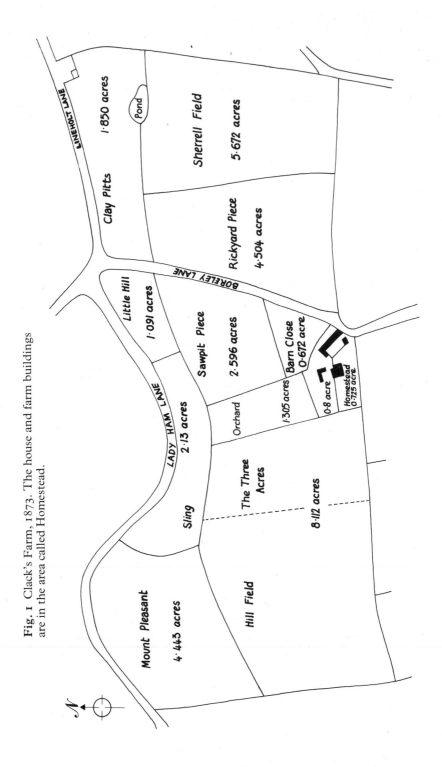

Fig. 1 Clack's Farm, 1873. The house and farm buildings are in the area called Homestead.

Mount Pleasant
4·443 acres

Hill Field

Sling
2·13 acres

The Three
Acres

8·112 acres

LADY HAM LANE

Orchard

1·305 acres

0·8 acre

Homestead
0·725 acre

Little Hill
1·091 acres

Sawpit Piece
2·596 acres

Barn Close
0·672 acre

Clay Pitts

1·850 acres

Pond

BORELEY LANE

Rickyard Piece
4·504 acres

Sherrell Field
5·672 acres

LINEHOLT LANE

N

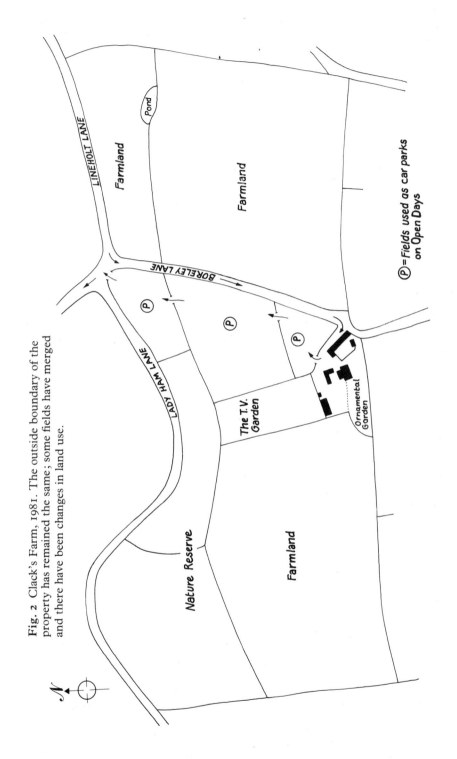

Fig. 2 Clack's Farm, 1981. The outside boundary of the property has remained the same; some fields have merged and there have been changes in land use.

LINEHOLT LANE

Pond

Farmland

Farmland

Ⓟ = Fields used as car parks on Open Days

BORELEY LANE

Ⓟ

Ⓟ

LADY HAM LANE

Ⓟ

The T.V. Garden

Ornamental Garden

Nature Reserve

Farmland

N

Across the lane on Rickyard Piece and Sherrell Field there was a poor crop of late drilled oats. According to the contract the oats were to be harvested and cleared by the previous owner. The crop was late to ripen; it was beset with many problems in addition to oat-eelworm, which had dramatically reduced the plant stand, the colour of the foliage indicated that the plants had been starved of essential nutrients. As with all poor crops which fail to cover the ground, weeds devoid of competition had run riot. On top of all that, field mice were everywhere, literally hundreds of them at every turn, Clack's Farm evidently suited them.

In October with the land cleared except for the stubble, we pulled out the hedge dividing the two fields, a not too difficult job with a tractor and a strong heavy chain. When 5th November came we had one of our many clearing up bonfires and as always collected up the wood ashes afterwards whilst it was still dry but cold and bagged it up against the time when we would have a use for it in the garden. Our plan for this now larger field was again to grass it down prior to using it for the poultry; there is no cheaper way of doing that than in giving nature a chance to help by way of a 'tumble down'.

By the spring of 1957 we were amazed by the overall emergence of an abundance of wild white clover. It started soon after the first weed-cutting operation with the tractor and mower. By mid-summer the field was almost solid with clover, its growth was lush, even the wild grasses were unable to compete with it. I was very pleased because I knew that clover in such quantity would do the land a power of good. Examination of a few roots showed that nodules filled with nitrifying bacteria almost smothered every rootlet—here was fertility being restored at little or no expense.

As all the land would not be needed for the poultry and what had been Sherrell Field was at the top of the sloping ground across the lane, I decided that it would be a good spot for some fruit tree planting. The ground had drained well during the August rainstorms, the cold air flow at blossom time would be going away downhill, so the risk of frost damage would be less than in the area lower down near the house.

At that time the Lenton Research Station was involved in work on apple and pear scab, diseases always more troublesome in the west than in the eastern part of the country. For research it is important to get an adequate amount of the disease in question in a trial. Worcestershire had a reputation for scab, so had 'Worcester Pearmain' apples and 'Williams' Bon Chrétien' pears. At Clack's Farm a trial would be completely under control with no commercial fruit growing factors or other people involved. We went ahead and planted two thirds of Sherrell

Field with two year old 'Worcester Pearmain' apples on Malling type 9 rootstock and the remaining third with 'William' pears on Quince A rootstock. After three years, apple and pear scab developed in a big way as it had a free hand in the control plots. At no time did we have any intention of embarking on commercial fruit growing, this was purely and simply a research project, a search for a practical answer to the scab problem.

The outbuildings
In relation to the land and farm buildings the siting of the house is almost perfect, we shall always owe a debt of gratitude to the person who decided originally to build Clack's Farm house where it now stands. We know that there has been a house on the same spot since the 16th century, the oak beams and brickwork in the scullery date from that period, as does the cellar with its sandstone walling blocks. We can only conclude that over the centuries there have been several partial demolitions and reconstructions of the house. Before our coming, the most recent one was in 1832 as recorded on a built-in stone tablet high up on the west-facing wall.

All the farm buildings with the exception of the Dutch barn are centuries old, built robustly in the traditional West country style with oak timbers collected from ships broken up in the Bristol area. Whilst these buildings are now covered with bitumen-painted corrugated iron, they originally had thatched roofs. The spars for the thatching still remain and we would like to re-thatch them all, but the cost would be prohibitive.

The black-and-white cow byre still stands firm with a single thickness of bricks filling in the spaces between the timbers, put there no doubt when the daub and wattle had perished. The old chains and rings hang loose from the posts; they have not been used for tying up cows since we came. The long, well-worn feeding trough has been boarded over to provide extra seating space for partakers of tea on our 'Open Days'. It could be said that we have done little to the outbuildings except to keep them in a reasonable state of repair. The one-up and one-down cottage, once used, according to the locals, for housing cattle-drovers overnight whilst their cattle quenched their thirst and rested, before resuming their journey on foot, has lost most of its bedroom flooring and is now used as a storeroom for our pots, seedtrays and composts.

The house
The 1832 date-stone built into the outside west wall can be misleading,

it was evidently put there during a reconstruction in the Regency era. The front elevation had the typical small Regency farm house look, an imposing front door in the centre with the five small sash windows built into the rich red local brickwork. When we took the place over in 1956, the front door looked the part from a distance but it was sealed inside and the outside stone doorstep was covered with weeds of the years. Although no footpath led up to the door there must have been one at some time to link up with the old rusty iron hand gate behind the cowbyre. Judging by the condition or absence of putty in the window frames, the neglect of the property went far beyond recent years. The 1832 reconstruction must have been a make do and mend affair, using such materials as oak beams from the demolition pile, as these were used to advantage inside. The back of the house escaped the 1832 purge and was left with its brick bread oven, original oak beams and open fireplace. More links with an older house were found in the cellar where the walls are built of large hand-hewn blocks of red sandstone.

Inside we were confronted with a dark kitchen, one tiny window facing north, an earth floor covered with sugarbeet sacks and walls that had recently been clad with asbestos sheeting to cover up the rough

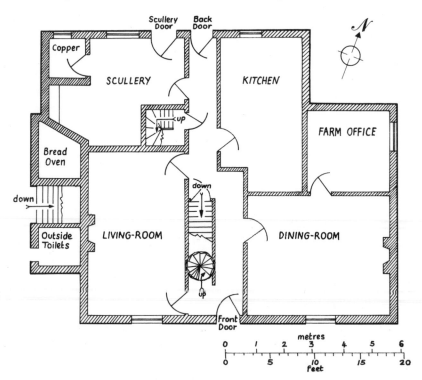

Fig. 3 House plan (ground floor), 1956.

brickwork. Fortunately piped water had been brought in during the last year or so—it came from an outside well.

The scullery had still got its low, well-worn stone sink; no doubt in past years milk pails had been washed here. The brick-built bread oven with its outside provision for firing was here, together with a large brick-built copper with a coal fireplace underneath. The large open fireplace, the enormous oak beam to carry the weight of the wall above it, the large hooks from the ceiling for supporting whole sides of home-cured bacon, all conveyed a picture of a past age when living meant work with a capital 'W.' The walls had been whitewashed at some time; the red quarry tiles on the uneven floor had seen better days. The scullery door which opened directly to the outside was a solid piece of farm-building woodwork with a latch to match, plus a piece of rusty chain inside to secure the door at night. With its coat of black farm paint it looked very forbidding.

The other back door a yard or so away did not look any more inviting. It led into a narrow dark passage from back door to front door without even a fanlight to transmit a glimmer of daylight—that was the centre of the general gloom. I just cannot stand dark corners in a house so it was all most off putting. Switching on a 25-watt light bulb it was possible to discern the steep narrow staircase, which led up to what I suppose was at one time the maid's bedroom. Further along this dark passageway another old wooden door prevented the unsuspecting from falling down brick steps into the cellar below. Then close by the front door, the steep spiral staircase wound its way upstairs (p. 29).

The so-called dining-room like all the other rooms suffered from poor light, the windows having been far too small. The open fireplace with its ingle-nook seats and pine overmantle had been ruined by the erection of a home-made brick fireplace to house a modern firegrate but the black painting of the pitch pine overmantle was nothing short of sacrilege. On either side of the overmantle were two farm carriage lamps, one with its thick glass on one side cracked and still carrying the soot marks of the days when candles were the only source of light to guide horse and family back to the homestead.

A massive iron gibbet for meat roasting was still in place. It could be swivelled to and from the fire as required. The brass clockwork mechanism was attached and still worked; its function would be to keep the joint slowly turning in front of the fire, a reminder that automation is not entirely new. I can still remember how cold and damp the dining-room felt on the day of my first visit, all the heat or most of it must have been lost up the chimney. Of course the undulating quarry tiles set directly on the damp earth did not help to improve matters, nor as I discovered later did the so-called adjoining farm office with its damp and ill-smelling atmosphere. Across the other side of the passage was the sitting room; it looked and felt unused. I was warned about the condition of the floor, which was as well as the drop to the cellar below was a risk to be avoided at all costs.

Upstairs a small bedroom on the north side had been recently converted into a bathroom with toilet; here again asbestos sheeting had been used to cover the walls.

Apart from the hay with its livestock of rats, mice and fleas we inherited in the maid's bedroom, the other three bedrooms were bare. The walls had been distempered and doors painted but the chilly, damp air from below pervaded everywhere. Some of this unwelcome air came from underneath the lean-to floor above the scullery. An inspection through a door in the wall of the maid's bedroom revealed timberwork that had been in place and part of the original Elizabethan farm house.

The purchase of Clack's Farm had landed us with a house that was not really fit for 20th-century living and certainly not good enough for me to ask Margaret to live in it—the risks to long-term health were too great to tolerate for any length of time. Within a short time we embarked on a limited house-improvement scheme which resolved some of the more pressing ground floor problems but with funds needed to develop the poultry breeding business this was all we could do for the time being, so in spite of some improvements life in the house was still far from comfortable. It was not until 1965, some time after the disastrous fowl pest visitation which ended Margaret's poultry breeding venture, that we were in a financial position to consider major house alterations. Apart from finance, the stumbling block in the way towards making the house attractive inside was the narrow passage way. We sought expert advice but it was not until an architect relative from Nottinghamshire came and sat down with pencil and paper and measuring tape that we learned that our ideas made sense and could be turned into reality.

Our first attempt came to nought. The architect's ideas and ours were in conflict; we wanted to retain the regency style of building with sash windows and could not compromise by allowing the introduction of another style, however limited it might be. Early in 1966 we made a new start with another architect, who agreed with our ideas and prepared the plans. All the existing windows were to be removed and replaced with sash windows three times the size, the window sills were to be lowered so that, even when lying in bed, one would be able to see the garden. The brick arches above the windows were to be cut and built as before, this resulted in a crisis when the builder said that no one was able to do a brick cutting job like that these days but our insistence was rewarded.

The addition of an extra bedroom provided the opportunity to increase the size of the lounge below. Now two large windows with low sills plus French doors enable us to virtually live in the garden whilst still protected from the weather, however inclement that may be. Taking out the front spiral staircase would be easy, finding space for the new one with easy treads more difficult. However, the architect solved the problem by transferring the front door to the back of the house alongside the scullery door. The back staircase was to be scrapped, the one time hay-filled bedroom was to become a dressing-room with its own toilet and washing facilities and we were to have a modern bathroom upstairs. Every door was to be solid with oak veneer, the staircase, back and front doors were to be made from solid oak as would be the woodwork for the door and screen separating the kitchen from the much-widened hall. We were more than fortunate as the builder had some oak on hand that had been in store for many years. It was so well seasoned that we did not have a trace of shrinkage when the central heating was started up.

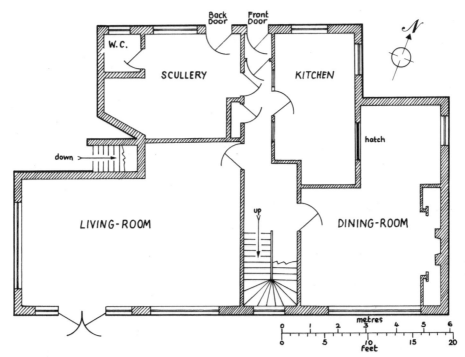

Fig. 4 House plan (ground floor), 1981. Note the extensions to the living-room and dining-room, and the elimination of the old front door and the back staircase.

The inside connection to the cellar was to be sealed off and new brick steps built outside. The outside brick-built toilet would automatically be demolished to make way for the extension to the lounge. These and many other alterations were itemized in the contract; the work was to be undertaken in such a way that Margaret could still live in the house. The contract specified that the work would be finished in five months, which turned out to be just about a year too optimistic. These 17 months were a period of great discomfort—Margaret stayed in the house without doors, windows and staircase until it became utterly impossible. Then, for a time, she made the best of it in one of the outside buildings before taking refuge in a caravan provided by the builder. It is one thing to plan to take an old house to pieces, but it is quite another thing when it comes to putting it together again. Crises occurred almost weekly and unexpected weaknesses were found. The back wall, with its two doors and windows, was much older than the rest of the house, and was found to be inches out of upright, so it had to be demolished and rebuilt. Floors previously thought to be all right were condemned and replaced.

The fireplace in the dining-room with its ingle-nooks, horrid black paint and ugly surround was not dealt with in the contract; at the time no one had any positive ideas. Margaret who had resolved the problem of the lay-out for the now much smaller kitchen, had some ideas and produced drawings which the architect translated into blueprints. It was to be a panelled oak front with the fireplace and hearth set back and surrounded with Honister slate to house a Rayburn open grate. This proved to be a great success. We still have ingle-nook seats and also well-disguised side cupboards to house bottles for human internal heating. The central heating was to be provided by means of a Trianco solid fuel boiler; it, too, has been a success even though it has meant manhandling the anthracite, which we store in quantity under the Dutch barn.

It is often surprising how people's opinions change. Before we started to reconstruct Clack's Farm house we were told that it would be impossible to make a silk purse out of a sow's ear. When at long last the job was done, the last lingering workman gone and after we had dealt with the scars in the garden, we were told that we were lucky to have such a beautiful home. If only they knew how hard that so-called luck had been won. After years of endeavour at last I was back in the country, with a garden and a house which combined to make a home, an environment for happy and satisfied living.

Considering that these alterations were planned and carried out before BBC 2 'Gardener's World' even thought about coming to Clack's Farm, it is surprising how well, without knowing, we anticipated our future needs. Without our own *en suite* bedroom, dressing-room and toilet facilities, our morning preparations on a recording day, when we have several people staying with us, would otherwise be a time of watching, waiting and hoping. I sometimes wonder why we went all out for a dining-room capable of seating up to 20 people when we were only a family of three. Looking back now I know that planning was done for us in advance—it all fits into the plan of finding Clack's Farm and making it what it is today. How grateful we are for such guidance.

CHAPTER FOUR

THE GARDEN

The way back to soil fertility

After years of neglect the whole farm was poverty stricken, putting 10.5 hectares (26 acres) of it down to grass and folding it intensively for some years with poultry did much to restore fertility. However this approach was not practical for either the ornamental garden or later on when the time came to reclaim the old derelict orchard, destined to become well known to viewers of 'Gardeners' World' as the television garden. In both cases there were masses of perennial weeds around after the clearance of the rubbish and old useless trees. Right from the start I decided that the weed and rough grass cover was too valuable to clear away and burn; in any case to attempt it would be too time consuming. So whenever an area was cleared, digging-in and completely burying the vegetation was undertaken, and I made a point of doing the job well, with no tufts of grass or a single weed leaf showing above ground. I tried to so plan things that the digging-in job was done early in the autumn but I waited for the ground to be reasonably wet, tackling bone dry ground this way can be hard work and give a less satisfactory result.

I contend that every plant takes valuable nutrients including trace elements from the soil and that it is folly to waste their stores by clearing them away and burning. Having buried the perennial weed roots and couch grass I knew that I would get a real crop of weed growth early in the following spring and it never failed to make an appearance. The first operation after the frost was a once or twice 'rake' over with a three-pronged cultivator to break up the clods; this in itself made a contribution towards weakening the weeds but more important it got the soil surface in the right condition for hoeing. Once the soil surface could be hoed I made it a rule never to allow the weeds the slightest chance to make above ground growth to replenish their roots. To some this may seem a hard way to clean very overgrown, poverty stricken ground but it works, by early summer the weed roots have always been exhausted and have died leaving us with an improved soil structure and some considerable uplift in fertility.

From this stage onwards we have always kept the annual weeds under control by regular hoeing, every time we have started the season with an enormous carry over of seed in the land but by persisting with the hoe and preventing weeds seeding we have kept on top of the problem. The system of folding the poultry breeding pens meant that their droppings went straight on the ground but there was no way of collecting the manure in bulk, so with no other livestock on the farm, the way ahead towards improved fertility in the garden was via the compost heap and to a limited degree with organic fertilizers.

Under natural conditions trees and plants return their foliage and in due time themselves back to the soil, the decomposition processes are accomplished by soil bacteria and fungi, together they convert the one time living matter into humus. We have used this end product, the humus of the compost heap, year by year to bring back the fertility of our soil. Only by composting every bit of useless vegetation, except the woody bits, has the present high level of fertility been achieved and maintained.

I have never attempted to make compost in a very short time since it is not only cheapest but also best to stay as close to nature as possible. For the long term return to fertility, we wanted well-made compost to be available in the autumn, that is the time for it to be dug into the land for maximum results. In the early years we usually had two or three compost heaps on the go at the same time. The procedure was simple; heaps were built up with mixed waste vegetation, the more varied the material the better I liked it. The heaps started with a 18 cm (7 in) layer of material laid directly on the soil, this was trampled down a little before applying a light dusting of garden lime, then the next 18 cm (7 in) layer of vegetable material went on top. After an attempt at some consolidation this second layer received a few handfuls of garden soil. As more material became available additional layers were added with the garden lime and garden soil treatment being applied to alternate layers.

Heaps started one autumn were ready the following autumn. The heaps were not covered giving the rain a chance to play its part in the gradual breakdown processes. The addition of the garden lime kept the heap from becoming a slimy mess, a common problem when too many lawn mowings are added. The garden soil supplied the soil bacteria and fungi to revel in the heap and help in the breakdown processes. These heaps started out with a base of about 1.8 × 1.2 m (6 × 4 ft) but spread out as time went on. The blackbirds had a grand time in the spring

I

Three stages in compost making at Clack's Farm. (1) Bringing together collections of autumn leaves and green vegetable material. (2) Adding garden lime to the first 18 cm (7 in) layer, the next layer getting a sprinkling of garden soil, the sequence being repeated until the bin is full. (3) Emptying a bin of some well-rotted compost, the sort that brought fertility back to Clack's Farm. (Note the next load of 'starting' material in the foreground.)

searching for worms, their scratching around made the compost heaps look very untidy but the compost was still good and the quantity made increased year by year.

With the coming of 'Gardeners' World' we tidied up by using wire-netting surrounds and corner stakes to prevent the heaps from spreading and looking untidy. Nevertheless we kept this fertility production area behind a fence out of sight of the cameras. When Barrie Edgar became 'Gardener's World' producer, we soon learned that he was interested in compost making and to do the job properly Barrie designed our present compost bins which are $1.5 \times 1.5 \times 1.5$ m ($5 \times 5 \times 5$ ft), constructed with slatted timber sides, the front slats being removable for filling and emptying. All the timber used was treated with a wood preservative before construction of the bins and this has given them the benefit of a long life. We still stick to the same procedure for making compost and the same time schedule—for us

2

3

compost making is a simple but an essential gardening job. I often refer to our compost bins as the heart of Clack's Farm garden since without them the road back to poverty-stricken soil would be short.

When we first came to Clack's Farm there were few worms in the soil, now they are here in abundance to play their part, making their burrows, ingesting decaying organic matter and returning it to the soil. The fact that they have come back means that we are still winning the battle for increased fertility. On the debit side more worms has meant that Clack's Farm now has a high mole population but our cats have proved more successful than trapping. We do not believe in poisoning; our policy is live and let live.

As a supplement to compost we have, whenever possible, used organic fertilizers such as fish, blood and bone or meat and bone. These and others wholly or partly based on ingredients of organic origin are usually more expensive than inorganic fertilizers when compared on a straight analysis basis. However, our results with them have been so much better than the analysis predicts at any time. Maintaining fertility in our soil or in fact in any soil is comparable to holding a piece of elastic taught; if you let go it rapidly retracts, so we shall continue to make as much compost as we possibly can each year.

Cultivation methods

Starting from scratch on that exciting day in September 1956 and continuing up to the present time (autumn 1980) I have been fortunate enough healthwise to be able to do all the digging myself. At no time during the period have we had paid help in the garden, so it is true to say that the present Clack's Farm garden is the result of a family effort, aided on the way by good friends. The garden has evolved gradually over the years, each extension has brought in more rough ground to be tamed, whilst at the same time we have not allowed the reclaimed areas to return to the wild. Now we have probably reached the limit that Riet and I can maintain in good condition at all times of the year. Nearly 1 hectare ($2\frac{1}{2}$ acres) is a large area, especially when it is broken up into so many pieces for presentation on television. At no time during the 25 years has there been any spare time. Consequently every operation in the garden has needed to be effective, as anywhere in the world it is not the amount of work done that counts, it is the results obtained that count and gardening is no exception.

Every successive area of rough ground tackled has had its more than normal quota of couch grass, nettles, docks, thistles, etc.—to the surprise of many of our friends we dig them all in. That is stage number one, the digging needs to be done well and the perennial weed roots completely covered, this has always been an autumn job for me. I enjoy digging but I am very particular about my spade; for me it must balance correctly when I hold it, it must have a sharp blade and not be too heavy. A stainless steel spade looks good but in use I find it too heavy especially if the shaft is also made of steel. The weight and size of the spade determines the amount of digging one can do at any given time, when I start digging I want to finish the day without being exhausted or in the throes of back-ache. It certainly is one of the gardening jobs that has helped me to keep fit.

With the exception of that first hectic rush to get ready for BBC 2 'Gardeners' World' in 1969, we have fallowed the ground for a whole season after the first digging operation. We have worked on the principle that perennial weeds die of exhaustion if they are denied the chance to develop actively above ground. So in the following spring we have first broken up the roughly dug surfaces with a three pronged cultivator and followed up at regular intervals throughout the season with a hoe, at no time allowing the weeds the opportunity to produce above ground growth. By July or August the roots denied of all food have died, from then on we have been left with annual weeds only. Starting as we did with an extremely heavy load of annual seed in the ground, I knew that it would take several years to scale down the problem. Our most valuable hoeing has been done in February or early March, when sometimes we have been accused of hoeing clean weedless ground. A look below the surface at that time reveals the white threads of germinating weed seedlings, a run through with either a three-pronged cultivator or a Dutch hoe eliminates them very quickly, at least it does ours.

During the growing season we have kept the hoe going, never if possible allowing annual weeds to seed. Gradually we have reduced the *annual* weed problem without resorting to weed control chemicals, the use of which we felt would only introduce their own problems, especially here where we grow such a wide spectrum of cultivated plants closely together. Before tackling some particularly bad patches of couch grass I have occasionally used Dalapon with excellent results. The applications were made on dry days in late summer or early autumn, a time which allowed about six weeks to elapse before the ground was turned over. At the start we had some large areas of extremely tall nettles, an application of a nettle killer (2, 4, 5-T) sprayed on just as they began rapidly to extend their stems, worked wonders, killing off the roots completely.

The secret of success when tackling an untamed area of ground is to start at the boundary and work inwards—that is what I always do.

Another point is, delay planting small subjects until the ground is reasonably clean, I planted trees before the whole area was clean but I made it a rule to keep the soil around them free from weeds. In my opinion good results depend on the way in which the ground is prepared, availability of water and plant nutrients. On our soil weeds can be serious competitors for water during the growing season and be responsible for plant nutrient losses. I would hate to waste fertilizers on weeds.

Over the years we have been able to increase and maintain the soil fertility by making our own compost. Although a farm by name we have no livestock and since the end of the pedigree poultry era we have had no access to animal or natural manure. At the start the trees did not contribute much to compost making but now the masses of autumn leaves are invaluable. Until the introduction of Bio-recycler a compost maker for grass mowings, we did have a problem in finding enough other waste vegetation to mix with the grass mowings; now we compost the grass separately. We make our compost on an annual basis, emptying the compost bins at winter digging time, spreading it then is relatively easy and it gets worked into the soil as the digging progresses. Our most frequently used cultivation tools are a spade, a fork, a Dutch hoe and a three-pronged hand cultivator.

We have not resorted to power driven cultivators. Having tried one I came to the conclusion that our garden and myself are more suited to the spade. At one time I was used to horses, they stopped when you shouted 'Whoa!'. The cultivator I tried carried on and left me minus skin on one of my knuckles, and the spaces for clear runs were insufficient. Here at Clack's Farm we are out in the garden all the year round, only the weather keeps us indoors, our tools are kept bright and shiny by use. Any tools less frequently used would need to be kept cleaned and oiled, otherwise it is hard work for the gardener plus a job badly done in the bargain.

Planning and design of the ornamental garden

When after a couple of weeks I had recovered from the ill effects of consuming too many black plum skins, I started what was to become for eleven years an almost regular week-end routine at Clack's Farm, involving a 160-mile round trip from Nottingham and back. Sometimes the visits were restricted to a single day but more often than not it was an overnight stay, which began with an early start on the Saturday morning and finished with a late journey back on the Sunday evening.

Keeping a rough record I made the journey well over 500 times, with most of them directly through the centre of Birmingham. There were no M6 and M5 motorways in those days; avoiding Birmingham would have added another 15 miles each way to the trip. All but a few of the journeys were uneventful. My rather crazy idea of transporting the 15 tons of Bulwell stone from our Nottingham rock garden in weekly consignments ultimately resulted in a broken back axle—it would have been cheaper to have hired transport for the job. Motoring along the same roads week after week made it an automated exercise with one's driving subconsciously related to traffic and weather conditions. On two occasions, in the very same spot, I was caught for speeding, the first time being singled out from a line of cars and lorries in Measham, Leicestershire, which I thought was unfair, but the second time early one Sunday morning with no traffic about I went through a radar trap. Even the black cat for the farm which was travelling with me in the back of the car, did not save me; it only expressed its displeasure when the car stopped. Perhaps I should be thankful that these are my only two recorded motoring offences in well over 40 years on the road.

In the beginning the week-ends were taken up with preliminary ground clearing for we literally could not see wood for trees. A look at the plan of the farm dated 1873 (Fig. 1) showed that the house at that time stood in an area called 'Homestead'; it included the farm buildings and was about 0.3 hectare (0.75 acre). With this plan in mind it was possible to identify the boundaries now lost in the wilderness, some old rusty iron fencing rails evidently marked the west boundary. To the south it was easy since the hedge was the dividing line between Clack's Farm and the next property Broomhall Farm. On the east side towards the farm buildings a hand hewn red sandstone wall was to be the limit, or so we thought at the time. Deciding where the boundary was on the north side could only be guesswork, the seedling hollies, nut trees, brambles and nettles defied us. Whilst we would not have a plan on paper it was important to decide right at the start how large the garden was going to be. As expansion of the original Homestead area was only practical on the west side we put a line of wooden stakes down beyond the iron fencing to show where our new boundary would eventually be. From the beginning we had set our sights on a garden of about 0.3 hectare (0.75 acre), to do that we had to encroach a little way into the field beyond called The Three Acres.

The hedge between us and Broomhall Farm was at least 5 m (16 ft) high and spreading over almost a metre (3 ft) of ground each side of it, an examination revealed that it was 'best mixed'—thorn, holly, brambles, blackthorn with some well-smothered box in places. The thought then occurred that in the years past it might have been entirely box and that only neglect had allowed the invaders to take over. Here we would undertake a task of reclamation when time and energy allowed.

On the east side of the Homestead area between the house and the farm buildings, we discovered another box hedge. This one had not been neglected for very long; 'Old Charlie' apparently used to cut this one regularly after letting it grow quite tall during the summer, selling the greenery for wreath making during December. The clearance of the relatively small brambles and nettles would give it a chance of complete recovery, especially if we could find time to cut it before long.

Behind this box hedge the weeds were tall and strong; they were feeding well for here were the three rather roughly constructed septic tanks. Although the ground around them was very wet we did know that these tanks were working efficiently. Two thoughts then came to mind, here was a possible home for some bog plants and secondly, perhaps more serious, had the septic tanks been installed with official approval? We decided to locate the outflow. This revealed that it was piped away only to surface in the lane where it streamed away alongside the verge towards Broomhall Farm. After this discovery we were not happy until we were assured that official approval had been granted. Our visit to the Droitwich RDC offices must have started a reconsideration of the situation as very soon afterwards the lane was closed for a full scale sewer-laying excercise, for which we and our neighbours were more than grateful, as sweetness returned to the lane.

We soon found that the house was built directly on the sandstone and that the cellar beneath was cut into the sandstone. This stone is not far below the surface anywhere in the Homestead, and behind the black and white 16th century cowbyre near the lane it outcrops. In the cattle yard in front of the cowbyre it dips sharply and as a result of repeated cleaning out operations in the early years it had become a deep hole with bare sandstone bottom. Here I thought was just the place for dumping the derelict rusting farming equipment, I well remember later on committing a mangold pulper and a chaff cutter along with many other farm antiques to burial in the hole. I also remember how pleased we were when the council asked if they could have permission to use the cattle yard to get rid of spoil from a local road widening scheme.

It was during this initial detailed search that we found the dozen or so straddle stones, including one without a top. Unlike the present day imitations, these had been hewn from stone many years ago and in this case from stone far more durable than the local red sandstone. No doubt they had done duty in years past for stacking the corn and preventing rats getting up into the stacks. In farming circles, maybe, they were thought to be valueless, at least they were never mentioned at the time of purchase. The one without the top later became a stand for a lady's head in stone, carved maybe nearly a thousand years ago. Ralph Atkinson of Thurgarton found her in a muddy stream. Some say that her first home could have been a nearby priory, others think that she arrived from farther afield, along with other building materials. However, all agreed that she was probably one of Cromwell's victims, when many priories, abbeys and churches were despoiled, only for the works of art in stone to be used regardlessly for house and farm building. We treasure our lady with her serene smile, clothed in close-clipped ivy, her face turned towards the house imparts an atmosphere of quietness and peace, qualities which are so seldom to be found these days, even in a country garden.

I am a great believer in the importance of defining objectives before embarking on any project, now with some idea of the magnitude of the task ahead I asked myself several questions and at the same time mentally supplied the answers. The project was to provide the family with a garden, an environment for living and myself space to grow the plants I love and without which I could not be happy, so a sizeable garden would be essential. The size of the garden would be such that we could plant trees without the need to mutilate them before they reached maturity. The trees would be varied in such a way that their shapes and colours could provide, either as specimen trees or grouped together, a backcloth for all the other subjects I would eventually plant. At all costs I wanted to avoid having trees as a background looking like a lot of regimented soldiers, something that so often happens when conifers are planted in quantity, for this reason we chose deciduous as well as evergreen trees. We would plant flowering shrubs too, but neither they nor the trees would be sited in such a way that they would impede the view from the house. Another essential requirement would be to have something in flower during all the twelve months of the year.

Implementing the plan for the garden

Whilst it was going to be an obvious disadvantage to be living 80 miles away and only to be able to get down to Clack's Farm at the week-ends, there were compensating factors.

I was now on the brink of starting to make my fourth garden. The first one in Cambridgeshire had been on a kind, fertile medium loam, then came an attempt on one of the heaviest clays in the Evesham district, followed by a great constrast on the light bunter sand in Nottingham. In addition the seventeen years at The Lenton Research Station, which I had been privileged to start, plan and plant, were years of invaluable experience.

So when in September 1956 on a fine Saturday morning I filled a wheelbarrow with tools and trundled into the garden area of the future, I had some idea of the task that lay ahead. Even so I underestimated the time it would take before we could claim to have an area around the house that we could call a garden and be proud of it. September was a good month to start, tree planting time would be November to March and I felt sure that I could clear a sufficient number of circles 1.8 m (6 ft) in diameter or thereabouts for the job before the autumn. Whilst working without a plan on paper I had a mental picture of the ultimate lay-out, so the positions of the circles were carefully chosen. We were planning to plant trees in the best positions, some as specimens others to provide a living backcloth for the rest of the garden. I was flattered and somewhat surprised and taken back when a recent visitor commented on our good fortune in having bought a place with all the trees planted in the right places.

Each circle-clearing operation produced its own problems, sometimes it was wire netting, at other times it was old semi-rotted farmhorse harnesses and there were also pighuts, troughs, etc. for good measure, all buried among the nettles and brambles. It was slow work, each barrow load was wheeled away to the big bare hole in the cattle yard. At the time I thought how convenient it was to be able to dump all the junk at such a short distance away. One week-end we had a real find— 'Old Charlie's' cider mill stone covered with moss. It was too heavy to move by hand, perhaps 250 kg (5 cwt) or more; it was a job that would have to wait for Bert's help.

In any case we would need both Bert and Marie's help very soon to pull out a row of hazelnut trees; the trees were 'old stagers' and only a tractor and chain would get them out complete with trunks and roots. That week-end was a busy one, Marie on the tractor and Bert operating the chain. At the start we dug around and cut through some of the larger roots, then came the tractor pull which was usually successful first time. That part of the job proved to be relatively easy but it took quite awhile even with three woodman's saws going, to get the green wood into manageable pieces for storing and burning later on. We set up the bonfire of brushwood in a patch of the densest rubbish so that at the finish we were left with a quantity of dry woodash and another circle cleared.

Pressing on without missing a single week-end we were ready in November to plant the first trees; they were flowering cherries and crabs. The consignment of trees arrived superbly packed in straw, alas that very week-end the ground was frozen hard, too hard for either planting or laying in the trees. This was not such a bad thing as it seemed as it gave us the chance to get some tall wooden stakes and tree ties together. The trees were a housewarming present from a great friend of many years standing, Jack Matthews of Thurston near Bury St. Edmunds. Jack knew my passion for flowering cherries and he decided that Clack's Farm garden should reflect that love right from the start and it still does.

After eighteen months the central ground area was clear, the junk was either in the cattle yard or if it was too large it had been carted away to the local council tip. During the clearance operation we unearthed what had been an old stone wall running from the corner of the house almost to the front hedge. The stone was a motley collection of small pieces which later went towards helping to make up the drive. It was useful to have our own tractor and to be able to borrow a set of cultivators and harrows for the preparation of a seed-bed for the lawn, by the spring we had got it down to a fine tilth. The time of year was just right, all the seeds in the ground—weeds and grasses—would germinate immediately. They did and for a time it was a terrible sight, weeds galore until we went over it with the tractor-drawn Hayter grass mower. Repeating the operation several times during the season produced a sward of sorts, but it was truly a tumbledown. The regular cutting got rid of the annual weeds, we were then left with the perennial ones. These were dealt with by overall spraying with Lornox Plus, a product stemming from work done at The Lenton research Station. By the start of the second season the lawn was beginning to look respectable, the indigenous grasses were thriving, practically all the weeds had disappeared and to our surprise the surface was level enough for us to use a power-driven cylinder mower.

It was during this second season that with Bert's help we cut the boundary hedge down to size. Neglected as it had been for years we were tackling a massive task, one that necessitated the use of an axe, a saw and plenty of space for a good burn. Again we were fortunate as Bert was then farming the land next door. Before we could consider more tree plantings there were several old apple trees to fell. I insisted that no stumps should be left in the ground and once more the wood from the trees was stored for logs. It was a great joy to have apple wood burning in the hearth the following winter and whilst looking into the flames I felt a sense of reward for the labour involved *en route*.

After clearing away on the west side some more half-dead apple and plum trees, the garden area now merged into a grass field with its line of poultry huts in the distance. Here was the need for a hedge. We chose *Prunus cerasifera* 'Pissardii' (purple glow) and planted a complete line along the west boundary of the garden. The plants were small one year old's but within four years they made an attractive flowering screen.

After five years of intensive endeavour we were beginning to see some worthwhile results of our labour; the wide open space around the house was slowly becoming a garden, with shrubs and trees either established or in the process of settling down after being transplanted. The south boundary hedge was recovering from its severe cut back treatment and it now began to look more in keeping with a garden than a terribly neglected farm. Of course we made mistakes—the old mangold pulper and other antique farm equipment, bits and pieces that should have been treasured, and not buried beneath tons of soil in the cattle yard. It would have been better to have planted an ornamental flowering cherry variety such as 'Kanzan' instead of 'Accolade'. Some may frown on 'Kanzan' because it is the most popular flowering cherry but our bullfinches ignore it whereas 'Accolade' appears to be one of their favourites. The flower buds must be sweeter to their taste and this deprives us of our earliest cherry blossom. Fortunately we planted several larger budded but later-flowering, cherries which are left unspoilt by the unwelcome marauders.

All the flowering cherries took a few years to get established but now they greet every spring with mass displays of sublime beauty. In all we have a considerable collection, our favourites are 'Tai-haku' with its coppery tints of young foliage which show up the full glory of the single large snow-white blossoms; 'Ukon' with its bronze foliage to contrast against lime-buff single or semi-double flowers; 'Pink Perfection' similar to 'Kanzan' but more dainty and discreet; and 'Shirofugen' ('White God') our latest spring flowering cherry with its pendulous double pink buds which open to blush white and finally pink.

We have *Prunus avium* 'Plena' planted in 1965 as a specimen tree in the lawn. It has become a feature of the garden, at all times its shape is beautiful but in blossom time its beauty transcends everything in sight. We found a place for a standard Cheal's weeping cherry, *P. subhirtella* 'Pendula Plena Rosea'. For at least 10 years it struggled to maintain its few and ill-spaced pendulous branches but now after twenty years the head is fully furnished to carry its mass of double pink blossoms each April; a case of patience rewarded. The same could be said of an upright and fastigiate cherry, *P.* 'Amanogawa', which we planted to fill a gap in the hedge. It would be wrong to omit *Prunus subhirtella* 'Autumnalis' which gives us so much pleasure blooming as it does from November till early March. Frosts may destroy some of its blossom but afterwards it comes back again with more single white flowers and the odd small branch in the house over Christmas is a real treat.

To follow flowering cherries we planted flowering crabs, *Malus floribunda* for its deep red flower buds and pale pink blossom, *Malus*

Above: West end of ornamental garden in January 1980. In the round bed is a *Pyrus salicifolia* 'Pendula', left foreground, a red chestnut with a bay tree in left background.

Right: Hedge of *Prunus cerasifera* 'Pissardii' planted in 1967 at the west end of the ornamental garden (photographed spring 1980).

Above: The old, disused farm pump, now an ornament beneath a Wisley Crab in fruit, situated by the main drive (July 1980).

Below: The one time cattleyard with the 16th century byre in background. The weeping willow (left, mid-ground) was grown from a cutting.

Our water garden was developed in stages between 1974 and 1980, and was made and planted in front of BBC cameras for 'Gardeners' World' programmes. The fountain and recirculation of water is operated by electric pump (summer 1980).

Christmas (1979) arrangement of holly from the garden in front of a large log basket, within the dining-room fireplace.

'Profusion' for its dark red flowers and in addition we planted *Malus* 'John Downie', for blossom in the spring and fruit in the autumn. We also planted a 'Wisley' crab apple, again for its glorious deep red blossom and its large attractive dark red fruit. At the time we did not appreciate either the vigour or potential cropping capacity of this one; now its large red fleshed fruits are valued locally and by some of our friends for making a superb rosé wine. Even so we consign barrow loads to the compost heap where the majority are consumed by the birds. 'Golden Hornet' is a more recent addition; we love its upright growth habit and its annual show of small bright yellow fruits.

Looking back now and remembering the time when we planted the *Cedrus atlantica* 'Glauca', then a very small tree, the space allocated to it seemed enormous. Now, after 20 years, it stands a perfect specimen free from interference from other trees. It is more upright than most, possibly due to the fact that it lost its leader early in life following which we caned a lateral upright to take its place. A faster growing tree, *Sequoia sempervirens* (Californian redwood) came to us in the first instance as a seed attached to a 1962 Christmas card from San Francisco—it already towers above all the trees around.

From the earliest plantings and the positioning of the trees we now reap the benefits and pleasures. *Sorbus discolor*, a tidy upright tree with its brilliant red foliage in the autumn, is in full view of our lounge windows. In memory of a very dear friend C.H. Middleton we planted *Laburnum* × *watereri* 'Vossii', simply because C.H. gave us the tree we had in our Nottingham garden. It is not a particularly beautiful tree but its long racemes of golden rain mark the beginning of summer at Clack's Farm. Nearby in a little backwater we planted *Pyrus salicifolia* 'Pendula'. After a few years we cut out its lead and now twenty years later it is still a smallish tree with weeping branches of grey foliage, in keeping size-wise with its position. This is an ideal pendulous tree for a small garden, far more suitable than a weeping willow. Another weeping tree we planted more recently is a *Betula pendula* 'Youngii' (Young's weeping birch). We have given it a specimen tree position in the lawn where its graceful form is much appreciated.

In a damp, sheltered part of the garden I planted some camellias which have flourished but unfortunately they cannot be seen from the house. Nearby in a slightly drier position *Liriodendron tulipifera* (tulip tree) continues to grow still taller without showing any signs of producing a flower; we fear that our Worcestershire summers are not hot enough to ripen the flowering wood. It is impossible to mention all the trees, shrubs and plants we have found a place for at Clack's Farm—our aim from the start was to give each and every plant the best possible

Fig. 5 Plan of ornamental garden, 1981. Close observers will note that the L-shaped flower bed, to the left-hand side of the lawn in the ornamental garden in the jacket picture, does not appear in this plan. This is because the jacket picture was taken in the summer of 1980 and in early 1981 this part of the garden was re-designed (see p. 152 under Roses).

Key to plan:

1. *Prunus* 'Ukon' (Japanese flowering cherry)
2. *Sequoia sempervirens* (Californian redwood)
3. *Malus* 'Wisley' (flowering crab)
4. Pigeon loft (over); hound kennel (under)
5. Dutch barn
6. Garage
7. House
8. Farm buildings
9. Pigsties (disused)
10. 16th century byre
11. Entrance and drive
12. Beech hedge
13. *Prunus* 'Fugenzo' (Japanese flowering cherry)
14. *Malus robusta* (Siberian crab)
15. *Betula pendula* 'Dalecarlica' (Swedish birch)
16. *Cedrus atlantica* 'Glauca' (blue cedar)
17. Pool and rock garden
18. *Magnolia × soulangiana* 'Alba Superba'
19. Peat Garden
20. Rhododendrons and azaleas

21. Hazel nut trees
22. *Sorbus discolor* (mountain ash or rowan)
23. *Pyrus salicifolia* 'Pendula' (willow leaved pear) weeping form
24. *Laburnum* 'Vossii'
25. TV garden
26. Lawn
27. *Betula pendula* 'Youngii' (Young's weeping birch)
28. Alpine Garden
29. *Kolkevitzia amabilis rosea*
30. *Prunus avium* 'Plena' (flowering cherry)
31. Rock garden plants
32. *Liriodendron tulipifera* (tulip tree)
33. Camellias
34. *Malus floribunda* (flowering crab)
35. *Malus* 'Golden Hornet' (flowering crab)
36. *Salix babylionica*
37. *Populus candicans* 'Aurora' (a variegated poplar)
38. Box hedge
39. Tea garden
40. Pump

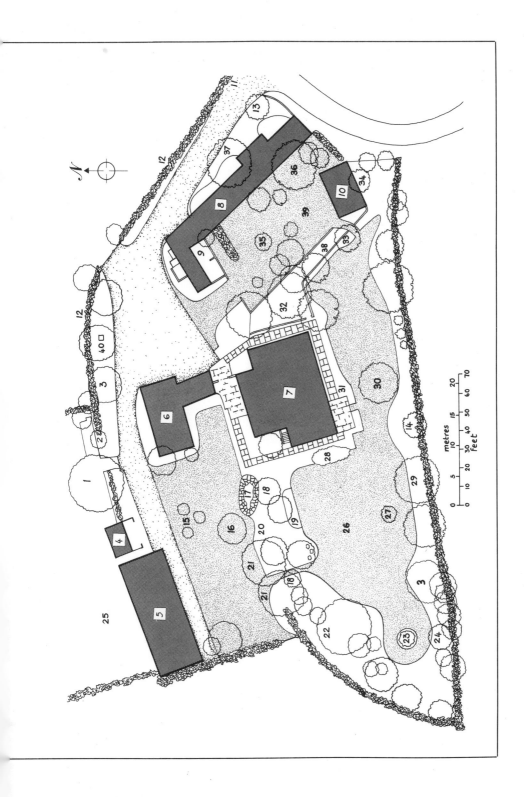

position together with conditions to suit their natural needs. We have endeavoured to plant as great a variety of subjects as possible to make sure that not a single day in the year goes by without some tree, shrub or plant being in flower.

With the coming of BBC2 'Gardener's World' alterations to the original plan have occurred. Will Ingwersen constructed and planted a gem of an alpine rock garden in two BBC 2 'Gardeners' World' programmes right in front of the lounge windows. It is brimful of treasures and gives us pleasure all through the year. The following season Will constructed a small peat garden close to his alpine garden. We expected the peat blocks to dry out and crumble but this has not happened. Now the roots of several of the acid soil loving plants hold the peat blocks securely in place.

We started in 1956 to create a garden, an environment for the family to enjoy in beautiful Worcestershire and this we have achieved over a period of 25 years. The garden has matured, the trees have grown up without the need to destroy their natural beauty by hard pruning. However skilfully pruning is undertaken, it never improves a tree's appearance.

Now we are privileged to share our garden with the viewers of BBC 2 'Gardeners' World' and our many Open Day friends. More often than not our visitors admire the roses, shrubs, flowers and bedding plants, but all too often the beauty of the trees that form the backcloth to the flowers and the garden escapes them.

CHAPTER FIVE

BBC RADIO AND TELEVISION

Early broadcasts

My first contact with the BBC came in 1938 when Mr. C.H. Middleton, that all time great of radio gardening programmes, suggested that I should act as his deputy whilst he took a six-week summer holiday break. The thought of being Mr. Middleton's shadow made me feel limp. Six half-hour weekly radio programmes would, I told C.H., be beyond me but he still put forward the recommendation. I was more than relieved when I learned that the BBC considered me to be commercially involved and therefore unacceptable. C.H. was very disappointed and thought again; this time it was Fred Streeter and how right the choice was, for the BBC and for gardeners everywhere.

A further twelve years elapsed before a young man from the BBC turned up at the Lenton Research Station with a small piece of recording equipment and suggested that I should make a short voice test recording. It was months before he came back to record a few minutes for a Midland gardening programme. The real break came when Boots announced the introduction of Chlorocide, a new acaricide for the control of fruit tree red spider mite, a Lenton Research Station discovery which was news of great interest to fruit growers everywhere. I made several recordings on the subject after which came the invitation to take part in several Midland region gardening programmes. It was at this stage that I started to join Percy Thrower on the radio. We had first met in 1940 when Percy brought a party of gardeners from Derby to see our demonstration allotment plots at Lenton.

This happy relationship continued when a new series of BBC television gardening programmes 'Gardening Club' started in 1954. My first appearance in front of the cameras in the Riverside Studios, London, was nerve racking; the programme was to be transmitted 'live' with me, a novice, to do a five-minute piece alone on chrysanthemums grown by Albert Parkes, the glasshouse foreman at Lenton. After several re-

Preparing a recording in a Birmingham garden; chrysanthemums grown at Lenton and transported in pots for the programme. BBC Gardening Club, September 1960.

hearsals I was directed to stand behind the table without moving more than just my hands to present a bloom of each variety to the camera at exactly the right distance and talk some sense about them at the same time. To my surprise both the producer John Furness and Percy were kind in their comments. I was far from happy as so much depends on a first effort in television.

However, I was invited back to show the then new tomato growing technique called ring culture. The viewers' response was such that six weeks later the programme was repeated. When BBC television garden-ing moved to Birmingham and 'Gardening Club' became a regular weekly programme, instant gardening in the studio started. How grate-ful I was each time that John Frisby always guided the Lenton 2-ton van with great care over the rough surfaces of the roads between Nottingham and the Carpenter Road Studios in Birmingham and sub-sequently to Gosta Green, otherwise our specially grown pot plants would have been ruined long before the end of the journey. In those black-and-white days, studio transmissions were live with occasional outside filmed pieces inserted, some of which were filmed at Lenton.

After a while Paul Morby the producer of 'Gardening Club' ceased to be satisfied with the limitations of studio gardening and took a long step forward by enlisting the help of the Birmingham Botanical Gardens' staff to develop a nearby area of derelict allotments into a television garden. At last the atmosphere of a real outdoor garden was on the screen. It was this experience with television cameras as opposed to film cameras for outside gardening programmes that prepared the way for a new BBC 2 'Gardeners' World' series, the first two programmes of which were recorded at Clack's Farm in March 1969.

Advent of BBC 2 'Gardeners' World' at Clack's Farm

In 1967 when I retired and left behind the facilities of the Lenton Research Station and the staff who had so generously helped me by growing plant material for television's BBC 'Gardeners Club' programmes, I concluded that my contributions to gardening via the television screen were at an end. In any case there was much to do at Clack's Farm. I was now living on the place and could devote more time to the garden—the basic work had been done but it needed the finishing touches and polish. By the end of the summer of 1968 I was well satisfied with the progress on the ornamental side but we were still without either a fruit or a vegetable garden.

However, I was giving thought to the matter when one day in September Bill Duncalf, the newly appointed producer of BBC 2 'Gardeners' World', turned up. Bill had been to see Percy Thrower the day before, now he was at Clack's Farm for a chat and a cup of coffee. Refreshed, we entered the garden by way of the French doors. The sun was shining and I was proud to show and tell Bill a bit of what we had done in the past twelve years. He agreed that it did present an achievement but there seemed to be a lot more to do elsewhere on the farm. Bill had noticed that it was only in the ornamental garden where acceptable tidiness prevailed, away from it there was still much left of the carry-over from the derelict days. We walked out of the garden under a canopy of nut tree foliage. Some nuts were already ripening and broken shells on the ground told the tale of raiding grey squirrels.

The almost empty Dutch barn and iron-fenced hound pen interested Bill. 'What were we going to do with them?' he asked. I did not know; at that time they were of little use to any of us except as a shelter from the weather. Surely no gardener could find a use for a four-bay Dutch barn—several years later I was proved to be entirely wrong. Moving on past a dense tall clump of nettles we stopped to look over an old farm gate, there in front of us was an old Worcestershire orchard with its massive pear trees, mostly 'Clapp's Favourite'. Some trees had in years past fallen and were now almost obliterated by brambles and nettles and much junk was still buried below the tall grass, weeds and brambles. Only in the foreground was the grass fairly short and green. Here was the limited area where Margaret had tethered her goats. To the right in the hedgerow was a large walnut tree, much sort after by a local timber merchant. Perhaps we should have accepted his offer as it was struck by lightning the following year.

We both leant on the gate, I commented on the nearby rather tired looking 'Worcester Pearmain' apple tree, telling Bill that the goats were hastening its demise. It was evident that Bill had ideas when he asked: 'What are you going to do with this lot?' It was a question we had asked ourselves, so my reply was short and to the point; 'Grow vegetables and fruit—varieties that have flavour, the ones that are seldom available in the shops'. Bill was silent for a moment and obviously in deep thought, then he said: 'Right, if you agree, we will record the first two programmes here in March next year'.

Here was a challenge out of the blue, an opportunity to do a couple of programmes from our own garden, without the support I had previously enjoyed. Could we do it? Yes, I thought we could but the time was short. It would have to be a rush job if both a vegetable and a fruit garden were to be ready for the cameras in six months. Then in a flash I was worried—Clack's Farm, I told Bill, is a name most unsuitable for television but he had another opinion, it was easy on the tongue and ear, and it was an unusual name that would stick. To avoid any future misunderstanding Bill warned me that vegetable and fruit programmes would most likely always be the Cinderellas of the series. We returned indoors to discuss the details, I drew a rough plan for the lay-out of the vegetable and the fruit sections, it was to be about 500 square metres (600 square yards) in total. It was agreed that I would erect a greenhouse. I preferred a wooden one and thinking of the future decided that a 6 × 3 m (20 × 10 ft) one with benching on both sides would be best. It was a few minutes after Bill Duncalf's departure before the penny dropped. We were again committed; the vegetable and the fruit garden had to be ready in six months and during most of that time it would be winter.

It was a challenge that demanded immediate action, that same afternoon I started with an axe and a saw and within a fortnight had cleared the agreed area of the few remaining trees and rubbish. Then I made a mistake I have not repeated since. To save time I asked Jim Gregg, our farmer friend next door, to plough the ground; this he did for love. Although he tried very hard, with the area so small, it was difficult to make a good job of it.

I levelled the site for the greenhouse and that involved moving quite a lot of soil, the whole area being on a slope. By Christmas the greenhouse was ready, the two rows of raspberries 'Malling Jewel' and 'Malling

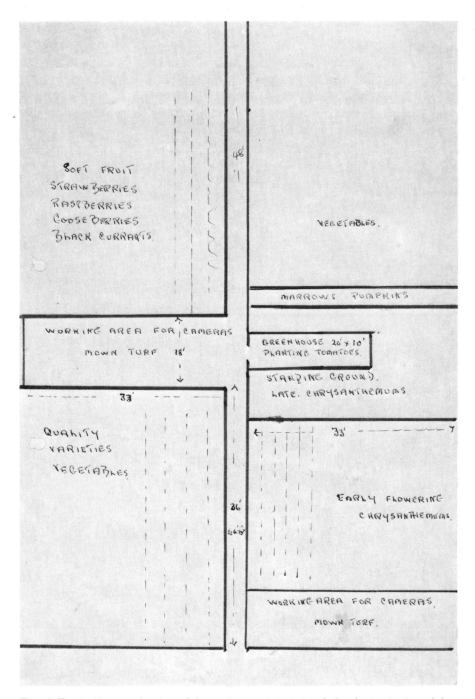

SOFT FRUIT
STRAWBERRIES
RASPBERRIES
GOOSEBERRIES
BLACK CURRANTS.

VEGETABLES.

MARROWS PUMPKINS

WORKING AREA FOR CAMERAS
MOWN TURF 18'

GREENHOUSE 20' x 10'
PLANTING TOMATOES.

STANDING GROUND.
LATE CHRYSANTHEMUMS.

33'

QUALITY
VARIETIES
VEGETABLES

33'

EARLY FLOWERING
CHRYSANTHEMUMS.

WORKING AREA FOR CAMERAS
MOWN TURF.

Fig. 6 Facsimile reproduction of the author's original sketch for the beginning of the TV garden, drawn in September 1968.

73

Promise' planted, as also was a row of black currants 'Baldwin' and a row of strawberries 'Cambridge Favourite'. Then I made another mistake in planting in the first year a beech hedge on two sides of the garden. In the following years it had to be moved twice to allow the garden to be expanded. By early February I was becoming more confident that all would be ready on the day, the Radio Times photographer had been down to take some colour pictures but I thought it wise to have a check up with the producer. One day on my way to Nottingham I

The author, together with Percy Thrower and his wife Connie, and their daughter, Margaret, judging together at the British Timkin Show, Duston, Northampton, August 1977.

called in at the BBC headquarters in Carpenter Road Birmingham. We chatted and Bill appeared to be satisfied with my report; the shock came as I was ready to leave. Just as a reminder Bill remarked: 'You know that we have billed work on apples, pears and plums in the Radio Times?' Well, I did not know, in any case no provision had been made for them in the garden.

The chips were now well and truly down, I phoned Jack Matthews that night giving him a list of the varieties, together with the rootstock particulars, I had hastily compiled. Jack quickly grasped the situation and asked when did I want them delivered. My rather desperate answer was 'A fortnight ago'. Needless to say Jack did not let me down. There was no time to lose—I had to clear more ground, dig it and have it ready within a week for planting, an operation which included the first move for the beech hedge to another boundary line. We needed angle irons, wooden tree stakes, tree ties and wiring for the cordons, otherwise the trees would soon blow over. It all took time. The trees arrived by special delivery, and were in excellent condition all having been carefully lifted with plenty of undamaged fibrous roots. With Margaret's help—her eye for a straight line was invaluable—we got the planting done with a fortnight to spare.

The great day arrived, the BBC vehicles were due some time during the morning. The first crisis occurred when the scanner, an 11 m (36 ft) long, fixed-wheelbase vehicle had to edge its way between our gate posts with barely an inch on each side to spare. Once the four vehicles were parked we felt easier, the cables were rolled out, the cameras set up with waterproof covers over them and everything ready for starting the next morning. When Bill Duncalf, who was staying overnight with us, drew the curtains at first light that next morning he was confronted with a countryside glistening with snow. Fortunately the snow turned to rain and Bill withdrew his request for a supply of warm water to melt the snow. Soon after breakfast Bill had another shock; Percy was in bed with a high temperature. After a few minutes' thought Bill decided that he would appear with me in front of the cameras and John Clarke should take his place in the scanner. It was a cold recording session. The heavy cameras got bogged down in the sodden, poorly covered grass paths but in spite of all this the first programme was in the can by the afternoon, and we then went into the warmth to celebrate. Next morning Percy had recovered sufficiently to make the journey from Shrewsbury, the weather was kinder and the second programme was recorded with less incidents. The BBC vehicles stayed overnight, a night when the heavens opened and turned Clack's Farm into a quagmire long before the morning. It was Jim Gregg's tractor that pulled them out and it was the expertise of the driver that got the scanner back on the lane through the gateway without a scratch. Nevertheless it was a very muddy crew that took the even muddier vehicles back to London.

A few days later we received a visit from the BBC's London Transport manager. He wanted to know more about this place Clack's Farm with its mud and narrow gateway. As a result of this first experience the gate way was widened to nearly double its original width, more ashes were brought in to make up the roadway and the grass paths gave way to concrete slabs. We shall long remember that first season with its ten programmes from Clack's Farm. We all gained a lot from the ex-perience of actually gardening in front of the cameras. All the sub-sequent developments and expansions of the garden stemmed from experience as we went along in the following seasons.

BBC 2 'Gardeners' World, 1980. The large vehicle in the right background is the TV Mobile Control Room (scanner). It contains the production control vision control areas, the sound control room and all the equipment to produce sound and pictures. In left background is the Video Tape van, which contains the additional equipment, not carried on this type of scanner, to make a video-tape recording on site. In the foreground is the security man's caravan.

CHAPTER SIX

THE DECADE 1969-1980

Planning, planting and sowing for television

The opportunity to make a garden for BBC 2 'Gardeners' World' was a real challenge, which I readily accepted but I had not expected Bill Duncalf to agree without further discussion to my lay-out plan quickly drawn up on our dining-room table. After talking over some of the details, Bill was all set for his return to London and the ball was now truly in our court. There was no time to lose if the agreed area was to be converted into a garden in six months' time, this was August and the first programme was scheduled for early March. The project needed more thought but as clearing the area was the first task I decided that that could wait and details could be worked out as we went along.

Being somewhat impatient by nature I could not hold my horses until the following morning, so out came a spade, an axe and a couple of woodman's saws. As I dug around that first old, but not very large, 'Worcester Pearmain' apple tree I had mixed feelings. For a start I knew that I was heading for trouble with the family as Margaret had a real passion for its fruit. The apples were small, beset with all sorts of pests and diseases and highly coloured due to an extreme nitrogen deficiency. Nevertheless they were always sweet and Margaret had the patience to peel and sort out the edible ones.

At the same time I was being reminded that 15 months earlier, I had retired with the intention of playing an active part in the activities of the British Crop Protection Council. In addition I had been engaged as a consultant on agricultural and horticultural matters by an international company. Apart from these commitments, I had allocated any spare time to be devoted to improving the already-established ornamental garden. Now, at this moment, without considering any curtailment to my other commitments, I was taking on something additional without knowing how much of my time would be taken up by this new venture. Advice and warnings were freely given by family and friends, it was said that I would wear myself out, that I should take life more quietly, etc. However, now 12 years later, the same friends comment on my wearability and all I can say is that gardening has been good for my health.

With all these thoughts in my mind I felled the tree, digging the trench and severing the roots, getting the stump and the roots out completely. Now I was over the first hurdle, I told Margaret that we would grow better apples than that old tree ever produced, although it would take two years to get the trees into cropping. With one or two other old trees out of the way and some clearing-up sessions I was ready but again my impatience got the better of me. As described above (p. 72), I asked Jim Gregg to lend a hand with the tractor. Through no fault of Jim's the result was unsatisfactory; it would have been better to have started with a spade in the first place.

It was a good thing that Jim's ploughing was restricted to the vegetable and fruit plot which was to be on one side of a grass path, as on the other side we had plans for a greenhouse which needed an undisturbed ground site. On this side the land was spade dug, here there was a tree that had to be left, it was a fast growing Californian coast redwood (*Sequoia sempervirens*). Away back in 1962 a friend received a Christmas card from San Francisco with three seeds attached, I sowed them and got two to germinate, the following year I planted one of them in a clearing just over the fence in the old orchard. In the next four years it had a rough time, competing with tall weeds and on one occasion it was even severely trampled on. Nevertheless it survived and by this time it was over two feet tall. Now, after 16 years, it towers above everything including the house and is still growing. Certainly not one of the best plants to have near the greenhouse especially on the south side but we decided to leave it. After all a greenhouse is movable, the noble redwood will easily outlive it and will continue to give pleasure and shade for many years to come, long after our time.

1969 was to be my first year of growing tomatoes in a relatively small greenhouse, previously I had been concerned with growing tomatoes in large greenhouses for research and development work, quite a different proposition. Sticking to my declared intention of going all out for quality, I chose 'Ailsa Craig'. I soon discovered that its faults are magnified when the plants are more confined: its spreading growth habit produced too much overcrowding for my liking and its tendency towards greenback increased but I managed by adequate ventilation to prevent tomato leaf mould. However, the crop looked superb on the screen. All the same for the amateur gardener we needed a variety more suitable for a small greenhouse but it had to be a variety with a flavour near equal to 'Ailsa Craig'. It was then that the search, tests and trials with other varieties began which finally brought 'Alicante' to our notice, a variety which seemed to have almost all the qualities needed.

Whilst our terms of reference in that first season did not include flowers, it was impossible for me not to think of having a houseful of tomatoes without plans for following on afterwards with late flowering chrysanthemums. The plan had provision for a standing ground, which in that first year was filled with chrysanthemums in 25 cm (10 in) pots. Unfortunately the 1969 BBC 2 'Gardeners' World' series finished before they came into flower. For the next three years I continued the time-consuming tasks of stopping, feeding, watering and disbudding for my own satisfaction without the viewers being able to share the pleasure of seeing the blooms.

It was a somewhat different story with early flowering chrysan-themums. They could be brought into flower from July onwards, so we incorporated these instead into the plan. Riley's of Woolley Moor and Johnsons of Tibshelf supplied the plants. It was great to be once again growing varieties carrying the family name, 'Gladys Billitt', 'Margaret Billitt' and 'red Margaret Billitt', a sport from the original. Alas 'Arthur Billitt' has virtually fallen by the wayside because, according to the experts it had too many petals and did not come up in the middle, in other words it was a flower difficult to finish. Now we have newer early flowering varieties with more constant performances outside and the exciting Pennine range of spray varieties which need far less attention during the growing season.

Coming back to fruit and vegetables we started off with two rows of raspberries, 'Malling Jewel' and 'Norfolk Giant'. Apparently many viewers were shocked when in March of that year we cut the canes down to almost ground level. I think that Percy was able to convince new-comers to gardening that this seemingly drastic treatment was really necessary to establish raspberries for cropping over a long period. 'Malling Jewel' retained its place from the first season, the yield was good, it threw its berries clear of the canes making picking easy and above all the flavour was excellent. After a few seasons we dropped 'Norfolk Giant'; it made a lot of canes, which were tall, and the berries were late to ripen, inclined to be acid and certainly had a poor flavour.

From then on we introduced several other summer fruiting varieties including 'Malling Promise' which is still with us. Many other varieties have come and gone for various reasons but mainly because the flavour of their fruit was not up to the standard of 'Malling Jewel' or 'Malling Promise'.

The introduction of fruit cages immediately increased our interest in growing more soft fruit. We started by growing a blackberry 'Merton

All smiles for the press—from the left, Bill Duncalf, the then producer of BBC 2 'Gardeners' World', the author, Percy Thrower and Barrie Edgar (19 June 1973).

Thornless' and an ordinary loganberry. We provided them with support posts and wires and in the second season they started to crop. As more space became available we tried other related berries and soon found that the youngberry was a superior version of the blackberry, with a brilliant black sheen and superb flavour. Alongside it we grew a boysenberry. This proved to be very similar to the youngberry with fruit slightly larger and with a touch of dark red in them. This planting regime gave us the chance to try out the blackberry 'Oregon Thornless', which proved to be a better cropper as well as being of superior flavour to 'Merton Thornless'. We also planted a thornless loganberry and after cropping that one, we scrapped the ordinary plant with its tiny thorns.

Then, in 1975, we planted a row of 'September' raspberries. Unlike summer-fruiting varieties, 'September' and other late fruiting varieties can be cropped the first year after planting. This row of 'September' was planted without protection from the birds; it fruited well and never showed any signs of bird damage. To this day the autumn-fruiting varieties in this district are virtually ignored by the birds—we often wonder why. We now have 'Zeva', 'Heritage' and 'Fallgold' added to 'September' and we can only think that Clack's Farm blackbirds prefer blackberries from the hedgerows, which ripen at roughly the same time in the autumn.

In that first season we planted a row of black currants, variety 'Baldwin'. From 1970 onwards it cropped well but sad to relate it is not one of our favourite fruits. However, nothing is wasted at Clack's Farm. Perhaps a word about surplus produce would not be out of place. Right from the start we have made it a practice to give away the produce we do not need ourselves. At no time have we sold any, for us growing for sale would take all the fun out of gardening.

Gooseberries come into the same category as blackcurrants, although we leave a small amount of berries on the bushes to ripen fully and these can be a treat. Our first row in 1969 was 'Careless', a popular variety but there are better ones. For those ripe sweet dark red berries we now have 'Whinham's Industry', a delicious fruit when fully ripe, also 'Leveller' a superb dessert gooseberry.

Right from the start our fruit growing was planned so that whatever would be shown on the television screen could be repeated in a small garden. We decided that fruit trees growing to a size that would ultimately need a ladder were out. This did not present any difficulty; our bush apples would be grown on either MM 106 or M 9 rootstocks, the pears would be on Quince A rootstock. Then came the choice of varieties, which should take care of the pollination in addition to supplying us with fresh fruit over the longest possible period. The cordon apples were 'Discovery', 'Golden Delicious', 'Egremont Russet', 'Spartan' and 'Orleans Reinette'. The cordon pears were 'Conference', 'Louise Bonne de Jersey', 'Doyenné du Comice', 'Merton pride' and 'Pitmaston Duchess'. Bush apples on M 9 and MM 106 were 'Rev. W. Wilks', 'Fortune', 'Early Victoria', 'Lane's Prince Albert', 'Red Ellison', 'Worcester Pearmain', 'Charles Ross' and 'Idared'. All these were maiden trees (one year old) and we could not or perhaps should not expect any fruit until the second year after planting.

This was where my impatience manifested itself again; I lifted five of our 'Cox's Orange Pippin' trees from across the lane. We dug them out carefully, in spite of their age (six years' old) it would be worth having a go, if we failed it could be a good story for the programme. They were on MM 106 and had made good growth after being planted as maidens five years before. To everyone's surprise they not only survived the move, but have now become well known in the programmes for their crops, both as regards quality and quantity. It is only by hard pruning that I have been able to contain them—if I had been patient they too would have been on M 9 rootstock.

The bush pears planted at that time were 'Beurré Superfin', 'Clapp's Favourite' and 'William's Bon Chrétien'. The three remaining old pear trees which we have kept for background purposes are all 'Clapp's Favourite' but are so large and tall that spraying is out of the question. Picking the fruit with a very long ladder is hazardous but the pears are by far and away the best for eating, cooking and freezing, far superior to any canned pears we have ever tried.

We also tried planting half standard plums, 'Rivers Early prolific', 'Monarch' and 'Victoria'. It was long before we had fruit cages and the bullfinch damage was such that we failed to get a crop, ultimately we grubbed them out and planted 'Victoria', 'Coe's Golden Drop' and 'Rivers Early Prolific' for training on a fence under netting; now we get both blossom and fruit.

This success encouraged us to try peaches, nectarines, apricots and a fig on another fence, we choose the varieties carefully for outside growing, one part of the fence faced south, the other part west, so there was a virtual suntrap. The varieties we thought were right were for peach 'Peregrine', for nectarine 'Early Rivers', for apricot 'Moor Park' and for fig 'Brown Turkey'. During several years of persistence and many hours spent each year training, feeding, spraying, etc., we did get some peaches and nectarines but never enough to justify persuading viewers to follow our lead, The apricots blossomed well in late February or early March but never failed to get frosted. Although we planted the fig in a 40-gallon drum, it never had sufficient root room and we must count this as one of our experimental mistakes. We tried various methods for controlling leaf curl on the peaches and nectarines without ever achieving complete success, we tried total coverage of the trees with plastic sheeting against frost and disease but finally abandoned the project as a bad job in 1978. We now have a 'Peregrine' peach in a large earthenware container, which in October is returned to a cold greenhouse to be brought outside again in late May, after the fruit has set, to a sunny spot on the patio. The space on the sunny fences is now allocated for planting in 1980 with the very best dessert plums and cherries.

Our efforts with wine grapes have been far more successful, in 1972 we planted two short rows, 'Riesling Sylvaner' and 'Seyve-Villard'.

They started to crop in 1975, an exceptionally good year for outdoor grapes, the summer was hot and long as was the following season. From both crops, Jean Laughton, the producer's assistant, produced a vintage white wine which she labelled Château Boreley. Since then the summers have been less kind but with the exception of 1978 Jean has had a good bubbling time each October and we have enjoyed popping the corks on special occasions.

At the end of each television season discussions with the producer have usually resulted in a further extension of the garden, new ideas and the introduction of crops and plants not previously grown. From time to time we have introduced the growing of less common vegetables; peppers in the greenhouse were an instant success. Outside, they interested viewers in the south and encouraged others to try growing them under some form of cloche protection. Aubergines with their attraction for greenfly have been kept in the background but having tried them outside with some protection from the weather, we feel that they may be a better proposition in the future.

Progress in the television garden

During 1969 BBC 2 'Gardeners' World' visited Clack's Farm on five occasions, each time recording two programmes. After a couple of visits the grass paths were replaced by concrete slabs to provide a weatherproof roadway for the cameras. At first a width of 1.20 m/(4 ft) made up from two slabs was considered sufficient. That was true as far as the cameras were concerned, but however careful they endeavoured to be, the operating crew were compelled to tread on the garden soil. It is not difficult to imagine the resulting problems, especially early in the season when we were trying to get the ground ready and in good condition for seed sowing and planting. Even Clack's Farm soil became unresponsive to treatment after two days of such misuse. Very quickly it was decided that the width of the paths should be doubled and these wider paths were laid, which made everybody happy, including ourselves. That season was a great experience, the viewers response to vegetable- and fruit-growing programmes was greater than had been anticipated. We soon discovered that it is one thing to grow plants but a totally different proposition when it comes to presenting them to the camera. Bill Duncalf the producer with his vast experience in television, had ideas which solved many a problem. For instance, as our 3 × 6 m (10 × 20 ft) cedarwood greenhouse was a standard amateur model, with a sliding door as the only access for the cameras, the possibilities for shots were very limited. It was frustrating to have suitable plant material on hand and to be unable to use it, so Bill with the co-operation of the green-

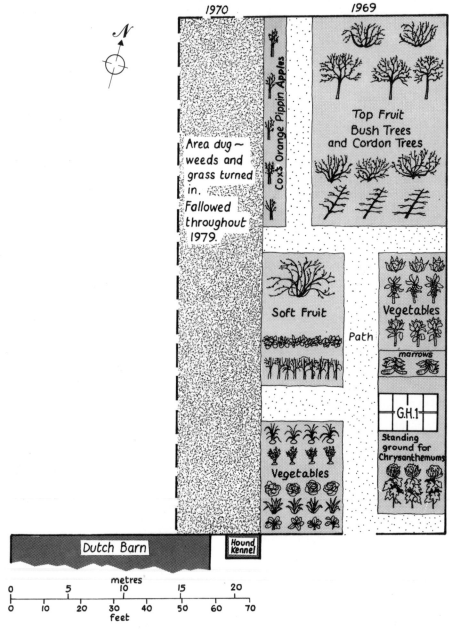

Fig. 7 The TV garden 1969–1970. The paths were of grass to start with but were gradually changed to concrete slabs to allow for mobility of BBC cameras. GH1: first greenhouse, 1969.

house manufacturers devised eight, removable, side-panel windows, which allowed the cameras access to every part of the greenhouse. Our outside planting distances produced problems, the space between rows of vegetables had to be such that the cameras could see clearly the actual plant under discussion, otherwise the viewer would only see a mass of unidentifiable foliage on the screen. To start with our two rows of raspberries were planted too close together, making it impossible for the cameras to get a view down between the rows. Fortunately this whole new garden area for television was well orientated. The greenhouse was easily sited east to west, which meant that it got the full benefit of the sun, as did the camera men with it on their backs rather than the reverse. This question of crop positioning is something that is important. With experience it has been possible to avoid plantings out of camera reach or in difficult light situations.

A 3.6 × 2.4 m (12 × 8 ft) aluminium greenhouse, a relatively recent acquisition, fitted with side ventilating panels which are removable for camera access. The floor manager (with shoulder strap), who has a radio talk-track receiver enabling him to communicate with the producer, is in discussion with the cameraman (striped pullover). On the left is a chargehand electrician, responsible for the lighting in the greenhouse, and the second cameraman. Cameras, larger: EMI 2001, smaller: Fernseh KCN 92 (April 1980).

Preparations for the second season were far less hectic. There was time to plan and everyone concerned, Bill Duncalf, Percy Thrower and ourselves started off with the advantage of the previous year's experience. The area for 'Gardeners' World' was to be as before but there was now going to be time for me to tackle some of the adjoining ground. I still look on these early days with grateful appreciation, remembering the skill of Bill Duncalf and his camera men, how they avoided showing on the screen the Clack's Farm wilderness beyond that small weedless, lush looking, vegetable and fruit garden on the screen! For the third season the television area was extended; there was now room for planting more fruit trees and soft fruit.

The erection of a second cedarwood greenhouse, plus a 1.80×1.20 m (6×4 ft) cold frame reduced the original vegetable growing area. This was compensated by the starting of a new vegetable plot on the land that had been reclaimed the previous season. With these additions it was possible to make more ambitious programmes on wider aspects of growing vegetables and fruit in home gardens. In April of that year we planted an asparagus bed but like all good gardeners we waited until the third season before cutting the first buds.

From 1972 onwards extensions to the television garden became annual events, and interest in vegetable and fruit growing mounted. It was necessary to increase the range of fruits—peaches, nectarines, apricots and a fig were planted on south and west facing fences, especially erected for the purpose.

The first three or four years of fruit growing for television were relatively trouble free, the bullfinches for which Worcestershire is renowned appeared uninterested in our fruit buds. Then it all happened. We grubbed up our orchard of 'Worcester Pearmain' and 'Cox's Orange Pippin' apples together with a large number of 'William's Bon Chrétien' pears. The bullfinches easy feasts were over; they now had to search for trees to attack and they found them. We tried many deterrents, all types of birdscarers but nothing short of overall netting did the trick. We now have four fruit cages with self-closing doors which, providing we check the netting at ground level regularly, are 100% bird proof. To overcome the risk of heavy snow-fall damage we have devised a procedure by which in the winter we roll the netting towards the centre, and there it is tied to the uprights until the swelling buds sound the bullfinch alert.

By 1973 our cleaning and clearing up operation had reached the boundary on the west side of the old orchard. The replanted beech hedge along the boundary was now about 1 m (3 ft) high. Here we thought was the opportunity to plant a shrub border. Percy made a plan

Fig. 8 The TV garden 1971–1972. Cedarwood greenhouse no. 2 erected on south side of first greenhouse. Area that was fallowed in 1970 now planted. GH1, GH2: green-houses.

1

2

Agriframe fruit cages. (1) In winter, with top netting rolled back and tied in centre, as a precaution against snow damage. (2) In spring the top netting is rolled back into position. Note the wide door provides easy access (May 1980).

Dave Chappel (third from right) together with other members of the Midland Branch in action on a new site for the National Vegetable Society's plot, Autumn 1979. Note that the ground is left rough for the frost to break it down.

and arranged for the delivery of the shrubs, some of which were planted in a programme, this was the beginning of what we now call the long border and what a joy it is now that it has matured.

The making of the long border marked the introduction of ornamental plants into the television garden. Soon afterwards a further extension provided space for a rose plot in which we planted varieties of hybrid teas, floribundas and climbers. The selection and delivery of the collection was arranged by the Royal National Rose Society through the good offices of the secretary Len Turner. This again was a landmark as collaboration with other specialist societies followed, with the result that we have been privileged to enjoy and benefit from the practical assistance of the Delphinium Society, the Dahlia Society, the National Chrysanthemum Society, the National Vegetable Society and, more recently, the National Carnation Society. With the exception of the National Vegetable Society, who arrange for the cultivation of their own plot, the other societies select the varieties, arrange for delivery, relying on us to grow and look after the plants throughout the season.

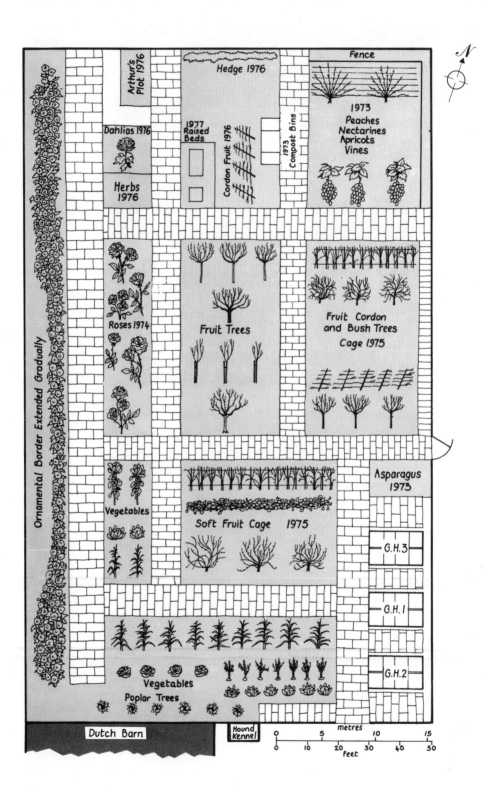

Fence

Hedge 1976

Arthur's Plot 1976

Dahlias 1976

Herbs 1976

1977 Raised Beds

Cordon Fruit 1976

1973 Compost Bins

1973 Peaches Nectarines Apricots Vines

Roses 1974

Fruit Trees

Fruit Cordon and Bush Trees Cage 1975

Ornamental Border Extended Gradually

Vegetables

Soft Fruit Cage 1975

Asparagus 1973

G.H.3

G.H.1

G.H.2

Vegetables

Poplar Trees

Dutch Barn

Hound Kennel

metres

feet

N

Whilst these additions to the garden were taking place there were other changes. Our dear friend Bill Duncalf retired in August 1973 and his place was taken by Barrie Edgar, himself a keen gardener. He loved the programme and was more than delighted when appointed as producer of BBC 2 'Gardeners' World'. In April 1975 Peter Seabrook assumed the presenter's mantle. Each change brought with it new ideas, and the garden was again in for another era of change and expansion.

Early in 1975 the National Herb Society was invited to plan and lay out a small old fashioned herb garden to demonstrate the growing of a wide range of culinary and medicinal herbs, but in the course of time and experience the plot is now entirely devoted to culinary herbs. In 1976 two raised gardens were constructed to show that even people confined to wheelchairs can garden happily, and that people unable to stoop can still garden, provided that the soil and plants are brought to within their reach. How well Andrew White, of the Nuffield Orthopaedic Hospital, demonstrated the extent to which disabled people can garden. His contribution in a programme gave fresh hope to the disabled and caused the manufacturers of garden tools to consider more carefully their needs.

Having started my gardening as a child, when at the age of six I was the proud owner of that 3 × 3 m (10 × 10 ft) plot, I have always had the urge to encourage both parents and youngsters along the same lines. A chat with Barrie Edgar and Peter Seabrook bore fruit—in 1977 we had two children's plots, exactly the same size as my first garden. It was a joy to see and hear Peter convey his enthusiasm for gardening to his own two children. Alison's plot was sown or planted entirely with flowers, often when time and conditions were far from optimum. Living in Chelmsford and gardening at holiday times at Clack's Farm was not easy. Roger had similar problems with his vegetables but their results were so good that both Peter and I wondered whether or not our rules for success were too precise.

The following year Barrie Edgar and the headmaster of Claines School on the outskirts of Worcester conducted a gardening essay

Fig. 9 The TV garden 1973–1977.
1973: Fences (north-east corner) erected. Peaches, nectarines and apricots planted. Vines planted. Compost bins erected. Vegetable plots extended.
1974: Ornamental long border started. Rose bed planted.
1975: Further planting in ornamental border. Fruit cages erected.
1976: Arthur's Plot and Herb garden started. Cordon apple trees planted behind compost bins.
1977: Raised gardens for the disabled built.
GH1, GH2, GH3: greenhouses erected 1969, 1971 and 1976 respectively.

competition which created a lot of interest, it was a surprise to us all when the winners were both girls, Alison Morgan and Rebecca Galassini. The reward for the winners was a season's gardening at Clack's Farm. Alison chose flowers, her reasons being clearly stated in her essay—she wanted natural beauty. Rebecca on the other hand was determined that growing vegetables for the family was the right thing to do. This time the distance to Clack's Farm was only eight or nine miles. The parents brought the children on Saturday mornings and on each occasion Riet was there to guide them. Tickling the soil with a child-sized, three pronged cultivator was a favourite weekly operation, it made weeding fun instead of a chore. If only the cameras could have captured the moment when, with a proud smile, Alison picked her first bunch of flowers to present to her mother or the surprised look on Rebecca's face when she lifted her first root of potatoes.

Another touching moment came when in 1978 Barrie Edgar brought Bob Roberts a blind gardener into the programme. We gave Bob his

BBC 2 'Gardeners' World' producer Barrie Edgar happily agrees with the author and Peter Seabrook to include the 'Rev. W. Wilks' apple in the programme, October 1979.

Bob Roberts, totally blind, whose contributions to BBC 2 'Gardeners' World' programmes have given so much encouragement to other disabled gardeners (photograph taken February 1978).

own plot to cultivate for vegetable growing. Although totally blind, equipped with his wooden measuring board, he was able to tell me that the plot we had given him was an inch out of square. Bob corrected the fault, making each corner a perfect right-angle before he started. Bob's contributions have given encouragement to the visually handicapped and help to those with blind relatives or friends. How often have we heard it said on an Open Day: 'If Bob Roberts can do it, surely we with sight should be able to get results as good as his'.

In 1977, Peter Wood, the editor of *Amateur Gardening* suggested that we should have a 6 × 3 m (20 × 10 ft) plot for growing a selection of vegetables. My first reaction was that it would be far too small but after Peter and Barrie Edgar had agreed to call it 'Arthur's Plot', I had no option but to give it a trial. I prepared a three-year rotation cropping plan and went ahead. To my surprise the retail value of the vegetables grown in that first year (1977) was £65.00 and what pleased me was that they were better flavoured than could be bought locally. Another immediate success was 'Mrs. Green's Kitchen Garden' which was the subject of a weekly article in *Amateur Gardening*. Although not shown on television it became a favourite with our many visitors. Here was a garden 9 × 7 m (30 × 24 ft) with a 1.5 × 1.5 m (5 × 5 ft) greenhouse, which, with its fruit, vegetables and ornamental plants plus a small piece of lawn could be related in size to many modern house gardens. The garden is planned and cultivated entirely by Riet who also wrote the weekly copy for the first two years under the name of Mrs. Green.

For the 1979 season the two 3 × 3 m (10 × 10 ft) children's plots were joined together to become an exhibition vegetables plot. The decision to go ahead with this idea came rather late in the spring but Dave Chappel, vice-chairman of the Midland branch of the National Vegetable Society, together with several willing fellow members tackled the task with zest and expertise. Out came the weathered soot and the dried seaweed, a good start to be followed up by all sorts of plant tonics, including a special brew of South Wales beer for the leeks. Dave Chappel, with his own brand of humour, was an instant success. His objectives were 45 cm- (18 in-)long runner beans as straight as a ruler, and 'Show Perfection' peas with ten peas to a pod. The fact that they were grown on cordons and that there were not many pods per plant did not matter; it was all a question of whether they would win first prize on the show bench. Leeks grown in drainpipes, celery in collars—it all looked strange at Clack's Farm but the viewing public and our visitors loved it, especially the bit about beer for good leeks.

On 31st March 1979 Barrie Edgar retired and John Kenyon became his successor as producer of 'Gardeners' World'. John shared the viewers' interest in large and perfect vegetables, so in October Dave Chappel made a start on a new and larger plot for exhibition vegetables.

Fig. 10 The TV garden 1978–1980.
1978: Mrs. Green's kitchen garden. Bob Robert's plot for the blind.
1979: Patio built. First National Vegetable Society plot.
1980: Some extra, smaller greenhouses, including 1.8 × 2.4 m (6 × 8 ft) one for Bob Roberts. Haywood family plots. Second National Vegetable Society plot.
GH1–GH7: greenhouses. GH4, GH5, GH6 and GH7 erected in 1979, 1979, 1980 and 1978 respectively. Sizes: GH1–GH4: 3 × 6 m (10 × 20 ft), GH5: 3.6 × 2.4 m (12 × 8 ft); GH6: 1.8 × 2.4 m (6 × 8 ft); GH7: 1.5 × 1.5 m (5 × 5 ft).

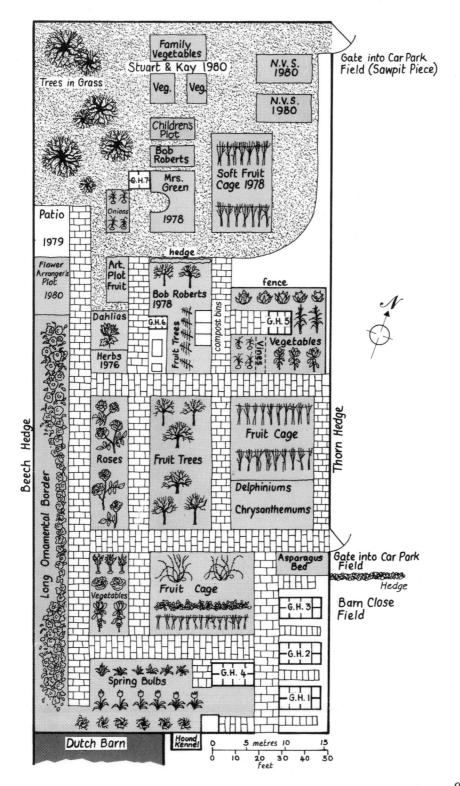

Trees in Grass

Family Vegetables

Stuart & Kay 1980

Veg.

Veg.

N.V.S. 1980

N.V.S. 1980

Gate into Car Park Field (Sawpit Piece)

Children's Plot

Bob Roberts

Soft Fruit Cage 1978

G.H.7

Mrs. Green

Onions

1978

Patio

1979

Flower Arranger's Plot 1980

Art. Plot Fruit

hedge

Bob Roberts 1978

fence

G.H.6

Dahlias

Herbs 1976

Fruit Trees

compost bins

G.H.5

Vines

Vegetables

Beech Hedge

Long Ornamental Border

Roses

Fruit Trees

Fruit Cage

Delphiniums

Chrysanthemums

Thorn Hedge

Gate into Car Park Field

Asparagus Bed

Hedge

Barn Close Field

Vegetables

Fruit Cage

G.H. 3

G.H. 2

Spring Bulbs

G.H. 4

G.H. 1

N

Dutch Barn

Hound Kennel

0   5 metres 10   15

0   10   20   30   40   50
feet

Again Dave was helped by a band of helpers from the National Vegetable Society. This time nothing was left to chance, the soot- and seaweed-treated soil had time to weather before the first programme in March. The fact that Dave Chappel travels up from Newport to Clack's Farm most week-ends during the season should be mentioned. His ambition is to get more gardeners to grow bigger and better vegetables. If talking and beer (not for drinking) will do it, he is well on the way to filling the country's show benches with superb vegetables.

Some friends of ours with a family of four children recently moved from Beverley in Yorkshire to Droitwich. Stuart and Kay Haywood have a very limited experience of growing vegetables, and as their home garden is too small for a vegetable plot, we gave them a 63 square metre- (75 square yard-) plot just across the path from Dave Chappel. Stuart solved the three-year rotation problem by dividing the plot into three roughly equal parts with grass paths between them and, with our help and encouragement, they are reaching the point of self sufficiency in vegetables. The two youngest members of the family Clare and Oliver were evidently itching to have a go on father's plot. Clare wanted space for flowers whilst Oliver had got his own ideas about vegetables. In order to satisfy all concerned Clare and Oliver were given a nearby small plot to share and now we have two junior budding horticulturists.

It is usual to build a patio close to the house where it can be used to the full whenever the weather is kind enough. At Clack's Farm it is different; for the purpose of 'Gardener's World' our patio is towards the bottom of the ever-expanding television garden. It was built early in 1979 at the far end of the long border, a convenient site for the cameras and for the incorporation of a well-established flowering cherry tree. Barrie Edgar's idea was to have a patio for demonstrating the potential of growing plants in containers large and small and this Peter Seabrook was able to do very effectively, including planting a peach 'Peregrine' bush tree in an extra large pot.

In 1980 John Kenyon increased the value of the patio by using it several times as a set for Sheila Macqueen's flower arranging contributions. Adjoining the patio Sheila has now her own plot entirely devoted to growing flowers and foliage plants for her flower arrangements; so ends the days when we searched all over the garden for suitable material.

The latest extension to the garden includes an aluminium 3 × 4m (10 × 12 ft) greenhouse, which Clay Jones used in 1980. Many of his contributions have been made with a small area in mind, comparable in size to the thousands of modern suburban gardens. To demonstrate growing greenhouse crops more easily we have also erected a 3 × 6m

Above: Inside a 6 x 3m (20 x 10 ft) cedarwood greenhouse. Note the propagator in background and, in foreground, a paraffin heater with extension flue (March 1980).

Right: Cordon apple Cox's Orange Pippin on Malling 9 rootstock, planted in 1976 (with the variety 'Discovery' planted nearby for pollination). Photographed in September 1980.

Left: View of the television garden, looking northwards, taken from the top of the Dutch barn. In the foreground can be seen a portion of the pigeon loft's roof and part of our new 6 x 3m (20 x 10 ft) aluminium greenhouse (spring 1980).

Below: The television garden, summer 1980, taken from a similar position as preceding photograph. Note Bob Robert's 1.8 x 2.4m (6 x 8 ft) cedarwood greenhouse in background (left); part of car-parking field shown right background.

Right: The day we celebrated our third wedding anniversary and made the 150th BBC2 'Gardeners' World' programme from Clack's Farm, 28 May 1980. From left, Peter Seabrook, Riet and Arthur Billitt, Percy Thrower.

Below: Gardening friends, seen here at the west end of the ornamental garden, share our celebrations on 28 May 1980. From left, Percy Thrower, Geoffrey Smith, Clay Jones, Sheila Macqueen, Riet and Arthur Billitt, Peter Seabrook.

BBC2 'Gardeners' World' cameras 'shooting' into the lounge where Sheila Macqueen is making a flower arrangement for the programme (May 1980).

A behind-the-camera scene while the author and Geoffrey Smith are in action in the ornamental garden. Note, left foreground, a VTR board and clock. Prior to shooting the camera is pointed at this board, thus identifying the tape. The clock gives a 'count down' to the beginning of the actual programme recorded so that, on transmission, the video-tape recorder is given the right time to attain the correct speed (May 1980).

(10 × 20 ft) greenhouse with double doors at both ends. This has fully automatic ventilation, which appeals to me—no more dropping of everything and running out the moment the sun starts to shine.

Throughout the decade we have tried to satisfy the camera's need for fresh material and ideas. Fortunately gardening is such a vast field that this has not been too difficult. The producers and all concerned have avoided resorting to gimmicks. For us it has been a privilege to participate for so long in a programme in which good gardening has been practised and nothing, not even failures, has been covered up.

Open days

Before we came to live at Clack's Farm in 1967 I was frequently asked the question: 'What are you going to do, buried in the lonely country lanes of Worcestershire, you will be so remote that no one will ever come to see you'. How wrong those forecasts proved to be. At that time I had no idea about television gardening—as far as I knew that was something that was going to end when I left Nottingham and when I no longer would have the privileged backing of the Lenton Research Station and its loyal staff. My reply to all these cheerless well wishers was always the same: 'I am a countryman; I have lived in a city long enough to earn a living', although it would be true to say that much of my time had been spent very close to the land and out in the wide open spaces of the countryside. Now on retirement I was going to keep my promise, leave the bright lights and go back to the fresh air of the Worcestershire countryside; this we did on the day I retired. It was television's BBC 2 'Gardeners' World' visits to Clack's Farm that proved the Job's comforters to be so wrong.

Although Clack's Farm is about 2 miles (3 km) from the A 449 Kidderminster–Worcester road and set in a complex of narrow lanes, regular viewers equipped with detailed ordnance survey maps began to find their way. In the first year it was exciting to talk to people who had seen the programmes and wanted to visit the garden. However, in 1970 the trickle became a stream, and there were so many daily interruptions that our gardening was in danger of being phased out.

By August of that year an Open Day was hastily arranged, maybe we could persuade the would-be visitors to come on a fixed date, a day when we would devote our whole time to answering their questions. Margaret prepared some direction signs and these she took out early on the Sunday morning, placing them in strategic positions at road and lane junctions. The garden was due to open at 12 o'clock; we were ready. Margaret, Bert and I sat waiting in the garage as the Clerk of the Weather had decided that it should be a day with more than a lot of rain.

The author, Clay Jones (centre) and Geoffrey Smith talk about window-box
gardening in general and in particular about a Rosemary rooted from a cutting, June
1980.

Geoffrey Smith (left), the author and Clay Jones in relaxed mood between recording
sessions, June 1980.

It was 1 o'clock before the first car arrived, by 2 o'clock their party was augmented, another two cars were parked in the paddock. Somewhat discouraged I went indoors for lunch, whilst I was off duty two weights and measures inspectors arrived to check our scales—they found it very difficult to believe that a farm in Worcestershire would open without attempting to sell something. During the afternoon the weather relented a little and the flow of visitors improved sufficiently for us to raise £50.00 for The Gardeners Royal Benevolent Society. Our first Open Day attempt was certainly amateurish but we learned a lot, experience that enabled us to make plans for more Open Days in the future.

As time went on BBC 2 'Gardeners' World' became more popular. This brought more visitors to Clack's Farm and we now needed traffic discipline in the lanes on the days we were 'open'. The local police together with Tom Lees, the Hereford and Worcestershire inspector of the AA, worked out inward and outward routes which the AA signposted; the system worked like a charm and hold-ups disappeared. Cars entered by way of our main entrance and left the farm via a gate three fields away. The local population is very long suffering on our Open Days, many of whom are unable to leave the lanes by their usual routes and have to find an alternative way if they want to go out. Some have solved the problem by coming in, either to help or to have a look around, some join the stream only to branch off at our gate.

As the number of visitors increased so did the number of helpers, all of whom to this day give their services free. The variety of people who help has been a great advantage. Very seldom are we without a doctor on our Open Days. A surveyor, who helped and advised us with the lay-out of the car park, found to his surprise, when measuring the field that a line of flowering cherry trees I planted 15 years earlier was not only the right distance from the hedge to give the head land needed but also the trees were the correct distance apart and could be used as markers for the lay-out of each double line of cars.

Open Days are happy days, all our helpers join in because they enjoy it and feel that they are doing something worthwhile. The weather has not always been kind but for some reason or other even a completely wet day does not seriously deter visitors from coming and our helpers have never let us down. It is a wonderful picture to see our car park attendants donning Wellingtons, sou'westers and waterproof clothing to go out and stand in the pouring rain one day and on another day in shorts and sandals, always with a smile. Some of our original helpers are no longer able to come but there have always been new friends willing and ready to fill their places.

Soon after starting our Open Days it was found, particularly on warm days, that there was the need for a drink and one of the ladies started to sell glasses of orange squash from the garage. Now we have a charming tea garden with white tables and chairs underneath colourful umbrellas. This tea garden is in what was once the cattle yard, between the old 16th century cow byre and the disused pig pens. Few will realise that, while they are having their cups of tea, underneath their feet lie buried the antiques thrown away years ago, when we were clearing what was then declared as Clack's Farm rubbish. It took Riet and myself only three years to transform this area, which was previously used as a dog pen, into this delightful small garden with roses, delphiniums and some shrubs. For several years some of the village people of Ombersley did the catering in aid of the village's own charities but unfortunately in 1979 they felt no longer able to commit themselves for another year and now the provision of refreshments has been taken on by our own group of regular helpers.

The welcome, refreshing cup of tea in the one-time cattleyard on a delightful, sunny Open Day, July 1980.

Several years ago we encountered another difficulty—toilet facilities. Up to that time we had visitors using our downstairs toilet but as the number of visitors increased so did the use of our water supply. On several occasions our borehole temporarily ran dry and we were left for twelve hours or so without water in the house, the input rate to the well being insufficient to meet the demands. Again with the help of friends, we erected a row of chemical toilets which to this day are adequate although somewhat primitive.

The number of visitors does not seem to depend a lot on the weather but during the last few years the numbers have been somewhat less mainly due to the high price of petrol; on the other hand coach parties have increased. As we are virtually unable to park coaches on an Open Day we found in 1977 that it was necessary to arrange special coach party days. After a few teething troubles with the parking of the extra large coaches we now find that most of these days run smoothly and people do enjoy coming with their friends and their societies. Now in the fourth year of coach parties we have had to decide to split the day in half so as to accommodate double the number of parties.

Apart from our five Open Days and six Coach Party Days, we have made one extra day available. This day is entirely devoted to disabled gardeners, not because we want to set them apart but simply to give them more space for their wheelchairs than they would have on or-dinary open days. This special day is completely organized by societies for the disabled and all profits of that day go to charities of their choice. It is a great privilege to be able to spend time with these people who, in spite of many handicaps, are so cheerful and keen gardeners.

Our lawns would find it difficult to endure an increase in our 20,000 pairs of feet a year and still look good. The desirable fine grasses gave up the ghost some years ago but the tougher indigenous grasses survive and given an extra bit of care they do seem able to suffer and yet still recover. Any other damage has only been very slight; check ups at the end of each Open Day have never revealed the loss of a plant. Cuttings have no doubt been taken with discretion or with permission. Some of our plants have arrived here by the same route so we cannot complain. On no occasion have we picked up more than a handful of rubbish, a tribute to the gardening public who respect a tidy garden.

All the same we don't think we could either cope with or want to have more Open Days a year. It is our home and we enjoy it to the full when it is quiet and we hear only the birds and the wind whispering through the trees—Clack's Farm is then truly a peaceful haven. As the result of Open Days we have made many friends, some so loyal that they come every time and if perchance they are unable to come they send us a

Open Day, May 1980. The first visitors start their tour of inspection. Vegetable plot in foreground with roses beyond.

Open Day, July 1980. The three cedar wood greenhouses, each 6 × 3 m (20 × 10 ft), were installed at various dates from 1968 onwards. The aluminium greenhouse, also 6 × 3 m, was erected in 1979. Note that Clack's Farm appeals to people of all ages!

postcard to apologize. They come from all over the British Isles. Four people came one Sunday morning in August, they had travelled over-night from Fort William, 568 miles away, spent the morning with us and travelled back the same day as they had to be back at work on the Monday morning. 1136 miles in 40 hours and they said it was well worth it!

BBC 2 'Gardeners' World' is truly an international programme; we have had visitors from the coastal areas of France, Belgium and Holland where at times they can receive the programme, and of course from Eire. The fact that our visitors come from far and wide and are nearly all gardeners has proved of interest to many societies, who are now reg-ularly represented on our Open Days. We would miss the societies now if they did not come. Perhaps I may mention the Midland Branch of the National Vegetable Society; not only have they had a stand here for the last four years but they organize the schools competition, an annual event sometimes in the form of a small vegetable show. It is good to see a young generation of gardeners being encouraged by the experts.

On Open Days visitors come prepared with questions and on occasions with specimens, some that cause alarm. Imagine my concern when a cauliflower plant with clubroot is brought out of a paperbag with soil dropping off it, or even worse the lady who insisted on having her bag of potatoes back after I had diagnosed potato eelworm as the cause of her poor crop. Needless to say both the cauliflower plant and potatoes were burnt without delay. It would be wrong not to mention Bob and Doris Roberts with York, Bob's guide dog. They always come and help us to prepare the garden for our Open days and are never absent on the day itself. For Bob in his dark world the opportunity to talk gardening with friends he has never seen gives him so much pleasure, that alone makes it worthwhile to have Open Days.

These Open Days enable us to meet the gardening public and maybe help them by answering some of their questions, it is a contact that keeps us in touch with problems which we may not encounter here at Clack's Farm. At the end of the season together with our helpers we feel that we have done something worthwhile, not only for the gardening visitors but also by being able to hand over the proceeds of the season to charities of our helpers' choice, so that the less fortunate will also benefit in a limited way from what gives us all so much pleasure.

Answering visitors' questions is no hardship for the author or his audience. Open Day, May 1980.

Part II

FROM SEED BED TO KITCHEN TABLE

CHAPTER SEVEN

ARTHUR'S FAVOURITE VEGETABLES

I have always enjoyed growing vegetables, maybe it is due in part to the fact that success is directly related to how well the cultivations are done. For me there is nothing more relaxing than a day's digging in the autumn when the soil is moist and the worms and small insects are near the surface to provide a feast for my companion the cheery garden robin. It is this autumn exposure of the soil pests that gives the robins a chance to help. Although their feeding is selective nevertheless many of the other pests, slugs for instance, are disturbed and their eggs lose the protection of damp winter quarters. Before Clack's Farm garden was regularly dug in the autumn we had plenty of snails and slugs, they both revelled in the piles of decaying rubbish and bred profusely under the shelter of old stones. No longer do our thrushes have their stone chopping blocks with piles of broken snail shells on the side—not to worry, their diet is still adequate as we have plenty of worms in all parts of the garden.

The repeated incorporation of well-rotted compost at autumn digging time has brought the worms back, always a good sign of soil fertility. To start with the organic content of our soil was very low. In periods of drought the vegetable garden suffered severely unless we resorted to frequent watering. Now the soil is far more moisture retentive and the cropping capacity has increased but not at the expense of quality in the vegetables. Flavour is related to the variety grown and I am only interested in varieties with the best possible flavour. It is always difficult to buy vegetables with real flavour, no matter how expensive or good looking they may be.

Commercially-grown crops are varieties selected for producing quantity with durability and good looks but seldom for flavour, so these commercial varieties are rarely of any interest to us. The way we make sure that our vegetables have good flavour is by choosing the varieties carefully, by building up the humus content of the soil (and compost does just that), and by using whenever possible organically-based fertilizers. It is this combination plus harvesting the vegetables when they are in peak condition that earns the gardener full marks when the dishes are presented at the table.

Peas

Individual tastes and preferences vary greatly but for me garden peas picked in June or early July, shelled immediately and cooked without delay are superb; if served with roast duck they are the ultimate. The season for top quality garden peas goes on until September and can be extended via the freezer to the whole year, provided that it is the right variety and the peas are picked young. Freezing does not add qualities that are lacking at the time of storing in the freezer.

We have given up sowing in the autumn or early spring round seeded garden pea varieties, simply because they lack the flavour of the wrinkled seeded varieties, which have a much higher sugar content and a more superior flavour, but they are more susceptible to the hazards of wet- and cold-growing conditions. We overcame this difficulty by sowing the seed singly in small peat pots in a cold greenhouse; once germination has taken place the plants can cope with the early season conditions outside especially if given some cloche protection to begin with.

I start by sowing 'Little Marvel', it is a real gem for quality and ideal for the small garden as it is only 45 cm (18 in) high by the time it comes into cropping, so needs very little in the way of support—a few canes and a strand or two of string are sufficient. Recently we have tried 'Fek'; the peas are very small and packed tightly up to ten at a time in small pods. Shelling can be tedious but the superb flavour makes this variety so rewarding. It grows to 75–90 cm (2½–3 ft) in height so needs a little bit more support than 'Little Marvel'. These two varieties 'Fek' and 'Little Marvel' are our favourites; we follow the early greenhouse sowings with successional sowings outside from mid-March until late June. The last mid-summer sowings can be followed with a mildew problem in September, but we get over this by spraying with benomyl before it breaks out. One other spray we use during flowering time; to prevent the little grubs of the pea-moth in our peas we use a vegetable spray of rotenone and quassia once or twice and this is certainly effective—practically all our peas come out of their pods undamaged.

We have tried sowing 'Kelvedon Wonder' as a late variety; it is known to be much less susceptible to mildew but its quality does not equal either that of 'Little Marvel' or 'Fek'. I suppose if large pea sticks were still freely available we would grow 'Alderman' but at 1.5–1.8 m

(5–6 ft) high it is not on at Clack's Farm; its flavour and tremendous cropping capacity must, I am afraid, continue to be a childhood memory. Riet keeps our rows of peas closely picked, never allowing any of them to get old. Those that are in excess to our immediate requirements go into the freezer without a moment's delay.

Riet has completely cut out blanching of any vegetables, having satisfied herself that much of the flavour is thrown away with the blanching water and that unblanched vegetables keep as well as with blanched ones. By dating the containers, the first in are the first out. Perhaps it is worth noting that we do not freeze any brassicas, not even brussels sprouts; we prefer these fresh from the garden.

Runner beans

Runner beans are a close second as my favourite summer vegetable and I like to be early with them. The plants are not safe outside until the May frosts have finished, so outside sowings have to be delayed until the beginning of May but by sowing in the greenhouse in $7\frac{1}{2}$ cm (3 in) pots I have plants ready as soon as frost danger is over. They are planted out on the top of a previously-prepared trench and they lose no time in getting on their way towards cropping. By growing them this way we are usually ahead of the rest by about three to four weeks. I think that it is a pity that the length of the runner bean has become so important; few of the new, very long varieties can compare in flavour and cooking qualities with 'Scarlet Emperor', my favourite variety for our own use. Here is a runner bean, an old variety, which responds to early planting out, which sets its flowers freely, and continues to flower and crop long after many of the newer varieties have finished. When picked young it freezes exceedingly well, keeping its flavour. For success with 'Scarlet Emperor' (and for that matter with any climbing-bean variety), prepare the trench well, putting plenty of well-rotted compost down below and a little garden lime on the sides. I do this before the winter weather sets in and, after exposure to the elements for several months, I fill the trench in. During the growing season, water thoroughly in dry weather and never use a high-nitrogen fertilizer—this will give you lush foliage but few beans. If flower drop occurs I water with a solution of a small handful of garden lime in two gallons of water, along the row.

French beans

We do grow dwarf French beans; they often crop just that little earlier than the runner beans, but we have now discarded the flat-podded varieties such as 'Canadian Wonder' in favour of the newer round-podded varieties which are so much better in quality. An early introduction 'Sprite' has been our favourite so far but we are trying several other round-podded varieties, including some from Holland. We have come to the conclusion that runner beans are far better for freezing than dwarf French beans, although we do freeze a small quantity so that we have some variety during the winter months. We will go on searching for a dwarf bean that freezes as well as 'Scarlet Emperor' runner beans, a good one would be a great find for the gardener with very limited space.

Broad beans

It would be true to say that broad beans are classed under our favourite vegetables but they have to be the right variety—broad beans more so than any other vegetable must have flavour and sweetness. Many varieties, especially those sown in late autumn or very early in the year, lack these qualities and are in our opinion not worth the effort of growing and cooking. As far as we are concerned there are only two broad bean varieties for the small garden, the 'Sutton' and 'Bonnie Lad'. Both are dwarf, produce good crops of small beans and they have the flavour that is not to be found in the taller varieties. As well as eating them fresh from the garden, if picked young they are an excellent choice for the freezer.

Potatoes

The Clack's Farm household is always critical when a new potato variety is served at table. If it is a first-early variety, 'Duke of York' and 'Sharpes Express' are the standard top quality varieties used for comparison. These are two old varieties now on the way back to popularity. They differ in flesh texture, 'Duke of York' being more floury than 'Sharpes Express', but both have that new-potato flavour lost to most, except as a memory, since the introduction of 'Arran Pilot' and the need for mint to provide a flavour of sorts.

There is more quality in some of the newer main crop potatoes. We like 'Desiree', a red skinned potato. It crops well, does not fall apart in the water when cooked and it keeps well, until the time when we start to lift our new potatoes. 'Gracia' is another of our favourites; its yellow floury flesh is packed with flavour. When it is served our guests, slimmers and all, always ask for a second helping. 'Vanessa' with its silky pink skin is probably the potato for the show bench but it also outdoes any other potato for baking in its jacket.

The curious shaped 'Pink Fir Apple' is our choice for a salad potato, the shape of the tubers is more akin to badly made sausages with nobbly pieces on them, than a normal potato—not to worry, the skin comes off easily after boiling. The flesh texture and flavour is unequalled for potato salad, but cooked and served in the ordinary way 'Pink Fir Apple' always has that new-potato flavour. Recently its cropping capacity has been dramatically improved. The virus diseases that it previously possessed have been counteracted by propagating seed from meristem cuttings instead of tubers. The seed-potato trade with the assistance of the research worker, has got rid of the virus problems which all but exterminated this classic variety.

Asparagus

Our luxury vegetable is asparagus. We established a bed eight years ago, and it was planted with one year old crowns of 'Regal' in April. The waiting period before cutting of two years was a testing time within the family. It is fatal to cut any spears before the crowns have fully established themselves; even now cutting is banned after 21st June and no cutting of fern during the growing season is allowed, however pressing the need is for fern for flower arrangements indoors. Specialist breeding has increased the size of the spears and the overall cropping capacity— the 'Regal' strain we planted has proved to be excellent. During the season we can eat asparagus with melted butter to our hearts content. The surplus goes into the freezer without blanching and on high days and holidays it comes out, when it still has the same delicious flavour as the fresh spring-cut spears. We would like a second asparagus bed but doubt if we want to wait another two years.

Sweetcorn

There was a time when I would have put sweetcorn in the luxury vegetable class, but now with some of the new F_1 hybrids producing good crops of cobs even in the not so good summers, we regard sweetcorn as part and parcel of our vegetable cropping routine. Again it is a question of choosing the right variety. After growing several different ones we now stick to 'First of All'; it is early and above all the cobs are full of flavour. We sow the seed singly in peat pots early in April and plant out a month later under cloches. It is this early protection for about a fortnight that gives the plants a good start, enabling them to produce several cobs per plant. Our sweetcorn is grown in a square block to ensure good pollination. When the tassels turn black we do a regular check to find out how the grains are maturing. The moment the white viscose fluid inside the grains solidifies, the skin of the grains becomes golden yellow, that's the time we gather the cobs—it is fatal to wait longer. Few vegetables freeze better than sweetcorn, we find it a great joy as a change from ordinary winter vegetables.

Brassicas

By the autumn our garden is usually well stocked with Brussels sprouts, savoys, curly kale and red cabbage; the last two are less used in this country but Riet, being Dutch, knows how to serve them. Kale should not be picked until it has had a little frost on it. Take the young leaves, strip the foliage off the stalks, cook it in a little water until tender, and serve with a knob of butter and sprinkled with nutmeg. Red cabbage is certainly delicious cooked with a couple of 'Bramley' apples and a few cloves, add sugar to taste. These are two vegetables to add variety in winter, both cheap and easy to grow but as with all cabbages we shred them finely before cooking and only use a little water for boiling them; this will preserve all the flavour.

My favourite winter vegetable is sprouting broccoli, by sowing both varieties, the early and late purple sprouting broccoli, we are able to pick over a long period, starting late February and in some seasons until April or even May. Picked in tight bud and served with melted butter sprouting broccoli comes a close second to asparagus, what more can you ask of a plant that is capable of surviving a severe winter, they recover after the severest frosts to produce such a tasty dish at a time when fresh vegetables are so often scarce and expensive.

Cauliflower to which the broccoli is closely related is a must for us, we are usually able to grow it 9 months of the year but to do this it is necessary to choose the varieties with great care. For successional sowings from early March onwards till the end of May I always use the variety 'All the Year Round', it has never let me down. For an early sowing in January we keep to the varieties 'Snowball' and 'Polaris', both do well on our soil. It is of course important to make sure that the young plants never get a check during the growing period, otherwise they just produce very small button like curds, not even large enough for one person.

Celery

We are very fond of celery, Riet likes it cooked but I prefer it uncooked when it is really crisp. As self-blanching celery lacks this crispness, we still grow our celery in trenches. It takes time to prepare the trench and care to carry out the earthing up by stages but it is worth it. 'Giant White' celery served with cheese and biscuits is a feast fit for a king, we grow it for an early crop and follow up with 'Giant Pink' which will stand longer in better condition and withstand the frost better. On shallow soils 'Dwarf White' is superb, it is crisp but shorter stemmed. For soups we grow celeriac, the stump rooted version of celery.

The author on bended knees to lift a head of trench-grown 'Giant White' celery, November 1979.

Onions

I enjoy growing onions, whether it is from direct-sown seed, sets or transplants raised in the greenhouse. On the table my passion is for fried onions, for this purpose the larger onions are best. I am not interested in showing large onions but I did get a lot of pleasure out of producing a 2.3 kg (5 lb 6 oz) onion in 1979, especially as it came from a batch of plants discarded when the National Vegetable Society boys had finished planting onions on their plot. For my own large onions I sow the seed on Christmas Day, and it is germinated in a propagating frame at a constant temperature of 18°C (65°F). For about a month after pricking out, the seedlings have to be content with the light from a bedroom window; heating the greenhouse for them alone would be far too expensive. By the end of February they are ready to recover in the better conditions of the greenhouse. By April the plants are hardened off and ready for planting outside. The prepared soil is rich with compost, as onions need plenty of good nutrients and must have a moisture-retentive soil underneath them. During the growing season our onions are fed with an organic fertilizer such as Back to Nature, the frequency of feeding depending on the size of onion I want. Varieties we grow for the large ones as well as the direct sown onions are 'Ailsa Craig', 'Improved Mammoth' and 'Kelsae'.

Leeks

Perhaps it would be true to say that I enjoy growing leeks more than eating them, although when they are served with a cheese sauce they are always acceptable. By sowing the seed early and planting out in a trench with plenty of compost below, we can grow some really large ones, especially when we start with varieties such as 'Giant Winter', 'Royal Favourite' or 'Improved Mammoth'.

The author lifting an 'Improved Mammoth' leek, fit for the show bench, but destined for the kitchen, November 1979.

A handful of fine carrots, 'Chantenay Red-cored Favourite', lifted by the author and Percy Thrower, BBC 2 'Gardeners' World', September 1974.

Carrots

Carrots come high up on my list but they must be tender whether young or old, have a red core and be full of flavour. It is not difficult to meet these requirements as so many good new varieties are now available. For the earliest carrots we start with 'Amsterdam Forcing' and then follow on for the rest of the season with 'Chantenay Red-cored Favourite'. Our battle against carrot fly (and the same goes for cabbage root fly) starts at sowing time with Bromophos in the seed drill and as soon as the seedlings are about $2\frac{1}{2}$cm (1 in) above ground we water with HCH. If we have to do any thinning out we do it in the evening and repeat the watering with an HCH solution.

Rhubarb

At Clack's Farm rhubarb is served as a sweet but I still count it amongst the vegetables. Many years ago I was fortunate enough in getting hold of a root of 'Champagne' rhubarb, it is a top quality variety but sad to relate long forgotten by the nursery trade, probably because it is not very suitable for forcing and is somewhat later than the newer varieties. We cherish our two clumps, the crop of slender sticks never fails to provide sufficient for our immediate needs and then some for the freezer so that we can enjoy some of it out of season.

Marrows and courgettes

I am not fond of marrow, it makes too watery a dish for me but courgettes, which are baby marrows, cut when young and tender are a different proposition. The variety we like best is 'Golden Zucchini', it never fails to crop from the beginning to the end of the season and if mixed with a green variety such as 'Green Bush' or 'Zucchini' it not only tastes good but looks most attractive when served as a vegetable.

Pumpkins

We usually grow a couple of pumpkins of the variety 'Hundredweight'. They are good to eat when cut young—no wonder the Americans adore pumpkin pie. We leave a couple of pumpkins on each plant for the children of our friends to use on bonfire night, and the bigger the better for that purpose.

Salad crops

Apart from our first row of lettuce and radish we tend to grow our salad crops between the rows of other vegetables as an intercrop or on the ridges of the celery trench. We love salads but we like our lettuces and radishes to be crisp, our favourite lettuces are 'Little Gem' and

'Fortune' with 'Cherry Belle' or 'Flamenco' radishes, both mild flavoured. Beetroot we grow over a long season, starting early in April and often pulling the last few roots in December. With seed sown at three-week intervals, we have a continuous supply of small tender beetroots, not only for salads but also enough for some to be served as a vegetable; mixed with a small amount of fried onions it is a dish worthy of a gourmet's table.

Cucumbers

Our cucumber for the early summer salad bowl is 'Improved Telegraph'. We have grown several other varieties in the greenhouse but all too often they have been disappointing on account of their bitterness or less crisp flesh. The all-female varieties often lack crispness and flavour but they are of course easier to grow. Outdoors under cloches or in a cold frame we favour 'Long Green' on account of its all round quality, including its cropping capacity.

Tomatoes

I have deliberately left tomatoes until last. I love growing them and enjoy some of Riet's tomato dishes and particularly her tomato soup made with fresh tomatoes but I have never acquired a taste for the fresh fruit. So right through the years I have relied on a critical family tasting panel for assessments of flavour qualities. According to the panel 'Ailsa Craig' is still the finest flavoured tomato, with several others including 'Alicante', 'Harbinger', 'Market King', 'Carter's Fruit' and 'Golden Sunrise' close behind. The reason why I favour 'Alicante' above all the others for a small greenhouse is because of its growth habits. It makes a compact plant, is short jointed so more fruit trusses are possible within the limited height of a small, amateur greenhouse, it sets its fruit freely from bottom truss to top of the plant, the fruit is free from greenback and we have never been troubled with tomato leaf mould on it. Grown outside 'Alicante' crops well, particularly if given the protection of the new expanding tomato sleeves made from perforated plastic film, when the fruit quality is comparable with the best from a greenhouse grown plant.

CHAPTER EIGHT

ARTHUR'S FAVOURITE FRUITS

Tree Fruits

As a young boy in Cambridgeshire with a large orchard close at hand I quickly discovered which of the apples, pears and plums appealed to my palate. At that time I did not always wait for them to be fully ripe and sometimes paid the price with tummy ache but I did find out that those that fell from the trees early with a maggot in them were usually the sweetest. I well remember the standard 'Cox's Orange Pippin' apple tree which stood just inside the gate; the fruit was small by present day standards but when fully ripe the flesh was firm and full of delicious flavour and juice. 'Cox's Orange Pippin' still remains my favourite apple but I have never enjoyed it as much as when it came off that tree, which I believe was growing on its own roots, at my old home.

Apples

Having always told would-be fruit growers that planting one year old (maiden) trees is the correct thing to do, for demonstrating fruit growing on television in the first year, we needed trees with an established branch framework, so I lifted five Cox's Orange Pippin apple trees on MM 106 rootstock. They had been planted six years previously and grown as bush trees. With the extra care and watering we gave them, they survived well, started re-cropping the following season (1970) and have done so ever since. Unlike the tree in Cambridgeshire they have their regular high-potash fertilizer feed in February or early March, and they are sprayed to prevent the maggots making the apples drop early.

When compiling the list of other apple varieties for the 1969 planting, it was naturally a catalogue of my favourite varieties, such as 'Red Ellison', a sport from 'Ellison's Orange' an apple with all its parent's good qualities, juicy, spicy and sweet flavoured and with a brightly coloured red skin. It is a dessert apple for September/October before the 'Cox's are ready and it is a variety less susceptible than most to spring frost damage, a good choice for Clack's Farm, lying as it does in the Severn valley.

At the time 'Worcester Pearmain' was my choice for a late August or early September apple. It is a dreadful, tasteless object if picked immature and stored for a while, but picked fully ripe off the tree and eaten straight away it is delicious. Having said all that here it has now been superseded by 'Discovery', one of its seedlings. 'Discovery' has everything that we could wish for in an August apple, good size, firm flesh with a superb flavour, something akin to 'Cox's and, although we prefer it fresh from the tree, picked fully ripe it will keep in good condition for a few weeks. Since we planted 'Discovery', the pollination of other apple blossom, particularly 'Cox's has improved dramatically.

The author pruning a dwarf bush, 'James Grieve' apple tree to open up the centre, December 1979.

'James Grieve' holds its position as a garden apple on account of its reliable cropping and its highly flavoured juicy fruit. It is a pity that it bruises so easily and does not keep but in September it is terrific—fresh from the tree we love it. Another September apple 'Epicure' is a real gem for the connoiseur, its flavour is superb; we can forgive it for not keeping for more than a few weeks. It is an easy apple to grow, with blossom resistant to spring frost damage.

'Lord Lambourne' just about completes my list of dessert apples. Having a preference for good flavour together with firm flesh, it is my first choice for an October apple when it is then at its best. A much maligned apple is 'Golden Delicious', simply because it is picked immature on the continent before being mass marketed in this country, with the complexion of a good apple but without any flavour. We grow it and

Winter spraying dormant fruit trees with Murphy's Mortegg to destroy eggs of various pests, December 1979.

wait until late October before picking it. The skin may be a little less beautiful than of those grown in France, but the flavour is really good and they keep in natural store until March or even early April.

When it comes to cooking apples 'Rev. W. Wilks' is supreme during September and October; in my opinion no other apple can compare with it baked, stewed or made into apple sauce. You really need two trees so that by de-blossoming one early on you can establish a rhythm whereby the biennial cropping problem is overcome. BBC 2 'Gardeners' World' can claim to have resurrected 'Rev. W. Wilks' almost from the dead, as it had lost favour many decades ago when lime-sulphur was the only apple-scab control product available—used on 'Rev. W. Wilks' all the leaves and fruitlets promptly dropped off. Now with such effective and safe fungicides as Captan there are no such unfortunate happenings after spraying.

For winter use it is impossible to beat 'Bramley's Seedling', it cooks and bakes so well and is one of the best keepers we can grow in this country. Its blossom can be damaged by spring frost especially in low lying areas with higher ground nearby.

Pears

It is impossible for me to write about pears without being reminded of the days when I ripened lots of 'Williams' Bon Chrétien' in the haystack. Picked mature but unripe and ripened in store it is a pear on its own but like most pears it has to be watched daily, otherwise you miss the chance of enjoying the fruit at its peak. The most difficult pear to grow is 'Doyenné du Comice'. It has the finest flavour of all pears but often cannot be grown on its own; at Clack's Farm it is planted as a cordon in the middle of a row of other pears to ensure efficient pollination. Recently we have added 'Onward' to the row, it is a relatively new introduction, the flavour is similar to 'Comice' and with us it crops more freely. 'Louise Bonne de Jersey' has an unique flavour which appeals to me when we can catch it just right.

'Conference' is a useful pear in its own right and can be grown on its own without a pollinator but when planted with other pears it is a good pollinator for other varieties. It may seem silly but I always want someone else to peel a 'Conference' pear for me, as they are so long and messy to handle when fully ripe but very acceptable flavour-wise. There is one pear we have inherited from the previous owners, 'Clapp's Favourite', a delicious fruit but unfortunately the trees are about 9 m (30 ft) high and it is impossible to spray them so most of the fruit are scabby. Luckily they are tremendous croppers and every year we get enough undamaged fruit for our own use, they are particularly good for freezing in a 50% sugar syrup.

Plums

The plum I have always wanted to grow again is 'Kirke's Blue' and now in the autumn of 1980 I have been able to plant a maiden tree against a south-facing fence for training fan shape. I know that it is a shy cropper but what quality when one is successful. The flavour is superb, the greenish-yellow flesh underneath the reddish-purple skin is sweet and juicy—that's my memory and I now wait for the dream to become true. Another superb dessert plum is 'Jefferson'. I have included it in our recent planting scheme. We have been cropping 'Coe's Golden Drop' for several years; its red spotted golden skin makes it look attractive and we like its rich sweet flavour. Ours is fan trained on a south-facing fence as a warm situation is essential for its success. There is still no greengage that can equal the flavour of the 'Old Greengage'; it is a shame that it is so erratic in its cropping habits. We have tried 'Cambridge Gage' as a sustitute, it crops more consistently but it is no equal when flavour is considered. The plum of the district 'Pershore' ('Yellow Egg') is a great one for jam making it crops when all others fail. We have inherited a tree of this variety in the hedgerows, which crops sufficiently to supply our needs.

Maybe for sentimental reasons we grow 'Rivers Early Prolific' and again it is a fruit with boyhood memories attached. It is the first plum that can be picked for a pie, but when fully ripe it is even better and I, for one, appreciate it as the first ripe dessert plum of the season. It is a small blue plum, amenable to be grown as a free standing tree, or trained on a wall or fence, provided it gets sunshine. Whilst the ever popular 'Victoria' plum is not on top of my list, we do grow it, in fact on a north facing fence where it does not get any sunshine at all and still crops consistently every year. In heavy cropping seasons we have to do some thinning out quite early otherwise the plums are inclined to be dry and small. A large well-ripened 'Victoria' makes a good acceptable dessert plum.

We are in the fortunate position that there is no need to plant damsons as there are so many growing in our hedgerows. This local damson is the 'Shropshire Damson', the small true damson which makes superb damson jam and the most delicious damson pie and for those who are partial to them pickled, they are the best. This true damson is far superior to the large plum-like 'Merryweather' damson which lacks the full damson flavour.

Peaches

Although we have recently given up growing peaches and nectarines outdoors at Clack's Farm, I feel that I should still mention the varieties that gave the best results under our conditions. The 'Peregrine' peach was a reasonably good cropper and we would grow it again if we were gardening further south where spring comes earlier. It is a quality peach with size, flesh and flavour to compare well with the best wherever they are grown. The nectarine 'Early Rivers' was our favourite, maybe because it did produce a crop. Although small in number the fruits were very good, being large, beautiful to look at, greenish-yellow flushed with scarlet, and delicious to eat. The reason why we discontinued growing them was that we did not get enough fruit to justify the effort of growing them. Our only hope is growing these fruits under glass and some time in the future we intend to have another go.

Grapes

Whilst not truly tree fruits, vines should be included. The best all round grape we grow in a cold greenhouse is 'Black Hamburg'. It is a good, reliable cropper and when grown well with the trimming done thoroughly throughout the season, ours produces magnificent bunches of luscious black grapes. To get the size on the individual berries some thinning is necessary. Next to the 'Black Hamburg' we grow a white dessert grape, 'Buckland Sweetwater', certainly less vigorous than the 'Black Hamburg', but hard to beat flavour-wise and the smaller crop from this vine is equally welcome. Our outdoor wine grapes planted in 1972 have been trained along wires and pruned more or less in line with traditional continental practice. We cropped them the first time in 1975, a summer remembered for its long periods of sunshine and high temperatures well into the autumn, ideal for ripening wine grapes. It was a vintage year as was 1976, again a hotter summer than usual. The only totally bad season was 1978 when autumn weather, with its cold and wet, came too early for the still immature grapes. Our varieties are 'Riesling Sylvaner' and 'Seyve-Villard', both white grapes. Although small, in a good season they are sweet enough to be eaten as a dessert fruit when fully ripe.

For me fruit growing is a challenge. There are so many factors involved, some of which are controllable, such as pests and diseases, the nutritional health of the trees, and the size and the shape of the trees. Then there is the unpredictable weather to contend with, which means that no two seasons are alike. It is a sphere of gardening where experience is invaluable and I have been fortunate enough to have been brought up with fruit growing from early childhood.

Fruit blossom time in late April or early May still arouses afresh my enthusiasm of past years, the sheer beauty of it all is so wonderful. By 21st April the cuckoo has usually arrived and is in full song. Spring has arrived but the only uncomfortable thought now is: shall we get through until the end of May without a damaging frost? Even if that does happen there will be another year to grow fruit at Clack's Farm.

Soft Fruits

Strawberries

The first strawberries we grew at Clack's Farm were 'Cambridge Favourite'. They were planted in September 1968, two rows of virus free plants, just right we thought for BBC 2 'Gardeners' World', which was due to start the following March. 'Cambridge Favourite' was and still is the most popular commercially grown strawberry, so plants are always available in garden centres and shops. It is a robust grower so, when plants are offered for sale, they always look strong and better value for money than those of other less vigorous varieties. 'Cambridge Favourite' is an easy and heavy cropper but for me the first dish of fully ripe Clack's Farm grown strawberries was a bit of a disappointment; they lacked the full flavour of ripe strawberries, which even lashings of fresh cream failed to improve.

There and then I made up my mind to get some 'Royal Sovereign' strawberry plants for planting in mid-August of that year. When they cropped the following July it was a totally different story. The ripe fruit was large and packed full of flavour, a taste that money seldom can buy, but the crop was light compared with that of 'Cambridge Favourite'. We still grow 'Royal Sovereign' for our own needs, its fruit quality being in a class of its own. I admit that it is a difficult variety to grow and that it is very susceptible to virus diseases. To minimize the problem we buy virus free plants and grow them for two years in isolation, as far away as possible from other varieties. After the second cropping season we scrap them and start again with fresh plants. To keep the chance of virus infection down we make sure that from the beginning of the season until the very end all plants are regularly sprayed for the control of sucking insects, as they are the spreaders of diseases. By digging in a goodly quantity of well-rotted compost before planting, even 'Royal Sovereign' can give a good account of itself. Compost not only holds the moisture the strawberries need so much, but also gives the basic supply of nutrients for healthy growth. Before the growing season starts in early spring, we clean all the plants up, removing dead and dying foliage, spray for greenfly and give the plants a feed with an organic based fertilizer.

Every September we put a score or so of plants in 12.5 cm (5 in) pots. They stand outside on the path until the end of February, when we tidy the plants up before bringing them into the cold greenhouse. As soon as they start growing, we feed them and spray them for possible greenfly. I always look forward to the annual treat of fresh strawberries and cream in April.

Recently we have tried with success putting eight plants into a growing bag, in which a tomato crop has been grown that season. We treated the bags in the same way as the pots and had a similar result. 'Royal Sovereign' is probably the best variety for forcing in this way but we have also used 'Tamella', another good flavoured variety. At one time our fresh strawberry season finished in August, but with the introduction of autumn-fruiting varieties, providing the weather is kind, 'Gento' and 'Rabunda' give us their fruits in September and October. By picking strawberries ripe and dry we have found that they freeze well and retain their flavour. Provided one does not expect the texture of fresh strawberries, they can be used in many ways during the winter months and make a welcome addition to the range of sweets one can prepare.

Raspberries

For me raspberries are an equal first with strawberries; again it is a question of variety. Fortunately we did plant in the first instance the best flavoured variety for summer fruiting, 'Malling Jewel' (along with 'Norfolk Giant', which is far behind if it is flavour that is wanted). 'Malling Jewel' in addition to its firm, superbly flavoured berries, has other qualities to commend it. The fruit is thrown clear of the foliage and canes, and consequently is easy to pick, and the plants do not produce a great surplus of new canes, thus easing their maintenance. Our fresh raspberry-and-cream season is an extended one, starting in July and finishing in November with the arrival of the first frost.

In late August/early September our autumn-fruiting varieties, 'September', 'Zeva', 'Heritage' and 'Fallgold' take over. There is little to choose between 'September', 'Zeva' and 'Fallgold' on the score of flavour, all are excellent. 'Zeva' produces the largest berries but they are rather soft, 'September' is a small firm berry and freezes well, 'Fall Gold' is a light cropper of small golden berries, and 'Heritage' is a very good cropper but its berries have a less pronounced flavour. Perhaps I could be forgiven for expressing a preference for 'September', a seedling raised in the U.S.A. at the New York State Experimental Station and introduced to this country by myself whilst it was still in trials under its seedling number. 'Heritage', however, has one big advantage over the other three varieties, the berries are firmer and much easier to pick in a wet season. These autumn-fruiting raspberries have been such a success at Clack's Farm that we should now be absolutely lost without them. For any gardener with a blackbird problem these could be the answer. For some unexplained reason they leave our autumn-fruiting varieties entirely alone, maybe because there is plenty of hedgerow fruit such as blackberries about at the time. However if we did not have complete fruitcage covering over our summer-fruiting ones, the raiders would be active from dawn to dusk.

Our fresh raspberry season goes on for at least four months and in a dry autumn it is extended to a possible five months; for the rest of the year our raspberries come from the freezer. Having more than sufficient for our needs during the season we can be very particular about the conditions of the raspberries destined for the freezer, they must be fully ripe and dry and taken to the freezer directly after picking.

Black currants, red currants, blackberries et al.
Whilst I can get really excited about the advent of the strawberry and raspberry seasons, my interest in other soft fruits is strictly limited unless they are presented in dishes minus their seeds. I agree that the extracted juices from black currants, red currants, blackberries, boysenberries, loganberries, youngberries and even Japanese wineberries can be used to advantage in many sweets but again success depends on the flavour, which is related to the varieties grown. When asked to recommend a blackcurrant for the small garden I have no hesitation, it is 'Baldwin' every time; it makes a compact bush, it crops well and the fruit has flavour and Vitamin C in full measure. Try home-made black-currant jelly with lamb—it is different, just right for my palate and maybe for yours. The more traditional red currant jelly is made here from the variety 'Red Lake', a tremendous cropper of large red berries, not only good for jelly but also for dishes made with the whole fruit.

Ordinary blackberry and apple pie is for me a troublesome adventure but stewed 'Bramley' apples with a thick, strained blackberry sauce is one of my favourite sweets. Picking the berries from 'Oregon Thornless' blackberry canes is an autumn pleasure instead of the ordeal it used to be when 'Himalayan Giant' was the garden variety. Our youngberries crop even more heavily than blackberries and if anything I would give them higher marks for flavour. It is a pity that they are not more widely grown—the shiny, black berries freeze superbly.

The Japanese wineberry is a relative newcomer to Clack's Farm. It makes a very decorative plant with soft red bristles covering the browny red canes and showing off its small brilliant red fruit. Riet acclaims the delicate flavour of the berries; for me there are too many seeds on them but, converted into juice, although the quantity is small, it is a useful flavouring for other dishes.

Gooseberries

I have left gooseberries until last simply because both of us are only interested in the occasional really ripe dessert gooseberry and then it must be a good flavoured one in the bargain. The ever popular goose-berry 'Careless' is alright for those who enjoy gooseberry pie, but for our dessert gooseberry it has to be either 'Leveller', with its large yellow berries or 'Whinham's Industry' with its red, sweetly flavoured fruit. On a warm day with the heat of the sun in the fully ripe berries, both are delicious. Just a handful at a time satisfies us, but even so that makes growing them as cordons worthwhile.

CHAPTER NINE

ARTHUR'S FAVOURITE SHRUBS

All the shrubs in Clack's Farm garden are there because we like them, and they have been selected and planted with the future in mind. Whilst most shrubs mature more quickly than trees it is important to give some thought to their positioning and ultimate space requirement. All too often shrubs are planted too close together, with the result that their full beauty and potential are never achieved, so we have endeavoured to allow our shrubs adequate space. Another mistake we have tried to avoid is the planting of subjects known to be too tender for our district or unsuitable for our type of soil. On other occasions we have wished to plant a particular shrub but have not been able to find an acceptable place for it. There are so many shrubs and varieties of them to choose from that it is a pity to plant without regard for their natural needs. The shrubs discussed are our favourites and of course a personal selection. They give us real joy right throughout the year but by no means is this list complete, as on many occasions, when we go to other gardens, we see shrubs we like and have not got in the garden—we often take a new look around to see if we can find a suitable place for them.

Starting with the maple, *Acer pseudoplatanus* 'Brilliantissimum' which we planted only four years ago. Until then we were unable to find a suitable, partially shaded position for it. Now its sycamore-like leaves unfold in the spring into a glorious suffused pink before turning green. *Amelanchier canadensis*, the snowy mespilus, is despised by some because of its popularity for roadside plantings, but here in April the bushes are smothered with white blossom against a background of unfolding pink-tinged leaves; then in autumn after the first frost we have a bonus of richly coloured foliage. By pruning after flowering we have been able to control the size of the bushes and obtain the maximum amount of flowering. *Arbutus unedo*, the strawberry tree, flowers with us in September or October. At that time the bell-shaped, heather-like flowers are very beautiful but we have yet to see it fruiting, as it should do at the same time from the set of the previous season's blossom. Although as a shrub on its own berberis is not a particular favourite of mine, as a backcloth for other subjects I find it unbeatable—the glorious coppery foliage of many varieties sets off other subjects and for that reason we have planted several of them.

Buddleia davidii appeals to us on two counts, its liberal display of immense panicles in July and August are superb to look at, and the flowers attract butterflies. It is a shrub that only asks for sunshine, type of soil does not seem to matter. We cut it back hard in February leaving only about two buds on the old wood and removing the weak growth entirely, doing this prevents it becoming leggy. We have three varieties: 'Black Knight', a very dark purple one, 'Empire Blue' the more common blue variety, and 'Royal Red'. The last is probably the least favoured by butterflies but we do appreciate its enormous purple/red coloured panicles.

Camellias

We are extremely fortunate that we can grow camellias. Our soil is virtually lime free and that suits them. Additionally we have been able to give some of them a damp, sheltered situation where the blooms are kept away from the early morning sun. Camellias are hardy, only the flowers being frost sensitive, but early exposure to the sun after a frosty night browns the flower petals. We have several varieties which are well established; for example 'Donation', well known for its free flowering and good growth habit. Each year in late March or early April it provides us with a fantastic display of large semi-double flowers of the clearest pink possible, so beautiful and perfect that our visitors have been known to doubt whether the blooms are real. Then we have 'Inspiration', the flowers being very similar to 'Donation' but a slightly deeper shade of pink. Our favourite single is 'Hatsu Zakura' with its large bright rose pink flowers with a prominent ring of yellow stamens—it, too, is very free flowering.

There are a few 'Williamsii' hybrids in the garden; they are not named varieties as they were given by a friend who did his own hybridizing. Last year we planted two white varieties, one double and one single but for those it is early days yet and it remains to be seen if they will do as well as the pink ones.

The blue spiraea (*Caryopteris* × *clandonensis*) is one of our small shrubs which when it is cut back very hard in March produces a wonderful

Above, left: The vegetable plot, planned on a three-year rotation basis, keeps the home kitchen supplied (June 1980).

Above, right: Visitors wait patiently for a word with Dave Chappel (centre), while another member of the National Vegetable Society gets on with the job (spring 1980).

Right: The author with 'Ailsa Craig' onions grown from seed sown Christmas Day 1979; the plants are kept actively growing by regular feeding and weeding (July 1980).

Our demonstration daffodil plot, with 25 varieties grown from Lincolnshire-supplied bulbs. In the background camellias, rhododendrons and azaleas add further colour (April 1980).

Tending the mesembryanthemums in the ornamental garden. Roses to the side and background are 'Lily Marlene' and 'Iceberg'.

A riot of colour in the television garden long border: crown imperials, daffodils, heathers, rhododendrons and azaleas, with a glimpse of magnolia 'Soulangiana' (April 1980).

Camellia 'Donation' in the television garden long border (spring 1980).

Above, left: The flower that started it all, just one pansy plant grown from a packet of 'Roggli Giant' mixed seed (summer 1980).

Above, right: Lilium 'Regale' in the television garden long border, grown from seed sown six years previously (July 1980).

Left: Riet tending a Begonia 'Lloydii' in a hanging pot — a single plant grown from seed sown in February (photographed August 1980).

display of violet-blue flower spikes from August until October, a time when blue is not too plentiful in most gardens.

Chaenomeles, the flowering quinces (more commonly known as japonicas) come in several varieties. We would like a bright red one such as 'Knaphill Scarlet' or 'Rowallane Seedling', but to date we have only been able to find room for 'Pink Lady' and it is a beauty—the crimson bud opens out to a clear rose pink flower, a wonderful sight in April.

Chimonanthus (winter sweet) was introduced to the garden recently by Sheila Macqueen; we should have found a warm sheltered spot for it long ago. From now on the prunings in the early spring will add beauty and fragrance to indoor flower arrangements. We were lucky that in the severe winter of 1978/79 our *Choisya ternata*, the Mexican orange blossom, survived as we would have missed its fragrant, orange-blossom-like flowers in May when it is in full bloom. It grows well in partial shade and at all times of the year it is an attractive shrub, roundly shaped with glossy leaves. After its main flowering period it still goes on producing flowers although in much less quantity until the end of the season. The attractive foliage has its own fragrance, which is an added bonus. We have learned our lesson and give it some protection in a severe winter to prevent die-back.

Another sun lover is *Clerodendrum trichotomum*, the 'glory tree', we added this to our garden recently so that we can enjoy its August display of fragrant white star like flowers and the china-blue berries that follow. A shrub we have growing happily in semi-shade is *Cotinus*, the smoke tree; 'Notcutt's Variety' was our choice. We chose it for its unique dark maroon foliage and so called 'smoke' which is a mixture of pink and purple wispy flowers occurring later in the season.

The only cotoneaster we have used in one or two places is *Cotoneaster horizontalis* (fish bone cotoneaster), to cover walls which never get sunshine. The scarlet berries in the autumn are particularly attractive against the old red sandstone wall near the gate.

We have several brooms (*Cytisus*) around the garden in a range of colours and sizes; providing we cut them fairly hard back after flowering they will be kept to a manageable size. There are many named varieties to choose from but we have grown ours from seed or from cuttings given to us by friends; so as far as we know none of ours is a named variety. Their life is not very long and we tend to renew them every three or four years so that they are always young and healthy looking in the garden.

Daphnes

One of the small shrubs we treasure in the garden during the winter months is the daphne; their flowering period is short but, as they flower in the bleak month of February, they are for us the first heralds of coming spring. We have *Daphne mezereum* with its sweetly perfumed purplish red flowers braving the cold, alongside *D. mezereum* 'Alba' with its prolific display of pure white flowers. We have managed to grow replacements of both from seedlings found near the parent plants. For real perfume of course the variety *D. odora* 'Variegata' is our choice, the flowers in clusters are slightly later and loaded with fragrance. We have given our two plants a sheltered position near the French doors and we can enjoy their beauty while we are sitting in the lounge. Again we are fortunate as daphnes do grow best in a well-drained, lime-free soil.

For June flowering it is difficult to beat deutzias—they are so generous with their show of blossom, asking little and giving so much but they do like sunshine. The varieties we have planted are *Deutzia* 'Mont Rose' with its large mauve/pink flowers and *D. scabra* 'Pride of Rochester', which makes a somewhat larger shrub with double white flowers tinted pink.

There should be a place for *Elaeagnus pungens* 'Maculata' (*E. p. aureo-variegata*) in most gardens; here its golden variegated leaves bring sunshine even on the darkest winter's day and it is also a very welcome addition for the flower arranger. We planted and had patience—it is a slowish grower. From time to time we have cut out twigs bearing all green foliage, otherwise the non-variegated growth would soon have become dominant.

Escallonias are one of the shrubs which are more difficult to grow at Clack's Farm, generally they are much happier nearer the coast. Earlier on we planted several, but from those only a single plant of 'Donard Star' has survived. With a little support it is trained as an upright in our border, where it gives us a beautiful show of pink flowers. We have recently added the variety 'C.F. Ball' to the garden and planted it against a south-facing white wall where it shows off its glorious deep red blossom.

Amongst the heralds of spring *Forsythia*, the golden bell bush, is probably number one; we choose the upright growers 'Lynwood' and *F. × intermedia* 'Spectabilis', but for many years the sparrows denied us the pleasure of their full glory by taking all the flower buds. Now that their habitat, an old wall thickly covered in ivy, has disappeared, the forsythias are back again in full bloom and we are once more back to routinely cutting out the old flowering wood in April to give the plants every opportunity for preparing a show the next year.

The only hardy fuchsias we have are 'Riccartonii' and 'Mrs. Popple'.

Although they are usually cut down to ground level in the winter, each spring they come up smiling to give us another show of dainty flowers from July till early October.

Many people despise *Hamamelis mollis*, Chinese witch hazel, as a common subject, but we admire its courage to flower in mid-winter. If the weather is mild the tiny curiously shaped yellow flowers are sweetly perfumed and a single twig gives scent and cheer to an indoor arrangement. A beautiful plant to visit in the winter whether it is frosty or mild.

A shrub which we have found flowers reasonably well in partial shade is *Hibiscus*, the tree hollyhock, but if we were replanting, a sunnier position would be our choice as they certainly would flower more profusely in that position. We have two: *H. syriacus* 'Woodbridge' with its large pink flowers darkening to carmine in the centres, and *H. s.* 'Blue Bird' with its blue saucerlike flowers—two magnificent plants.

Hydrangeas

For a prolonged display of flowers during the summer and early autumn in a range of blue and pink, hydrangeas take a lot of beating. With no effort at all we can grow the blues as our soil is somewhat acid but the pinks are not despised either. Hydrangeas are not too demanding as far as sunshine is concerned but do like feeding, shelter and moisture. In the spring we remove the previous year's flower heads and all the weak growth; to prevent legginess we cut back hard every third year. *Hydrangea macrophylla* 'Blue Wave' is probably our favourite with its large plate like blue flowerheads. *H. aborescens* 'Grandiflora' is a grand variety with large round heads of creamy white florets which turn bronzy brown in the autumn and remain so all through the winter; we have found it one of the most hardy varieties.

We do have a few dry sites in the garden and here we have some hypericums, the variety 'Hidcote' is outstanding with us, provided we cut it back drastically every other year early in the season. *H. inodorum* (*H. elatum*) 'Elstead' is the one for a succession of yellow flowers together with rose coloured berries—an attractive combination.

As June is a poor month for flowering shrubs we would not be without *Kolkwitzia*; every year we are delighted by the profusion of small, pure pink, foxglove-like, yellow-throated flowers. We have two shrubs, one flowers very freely in full sunshine, the other is certainly from a different clone which flowers less, but has the added disadvantage of being in semi-shade. We prune after flowering cutting out the old flowering shoots. It is fairly easy to propagate from an existing plant but do make sure that you get your cutting from a free flowering specimen.

We could not have a garden without lavenders (*Lavandula*) although they thrive better on a naturally limy soil. We grow a few, amongst them the variety 'Hidcote' by far the most strikingly coloured form, the deep purple blue with the silvery foliage providing a most beautiful contrast. We manage to keep it dwarf and tidy by pruning after flowering; the same could be said of 'Munstead', a slightly taller grower with dark lavender blue flower spikes.

We value *Lippia citriodora*, the lemon-scented verbena, for its pleasantly perfumed leaves. We have planted it in a narrow, south-facing border at the front of the house but it is rather tender and in spite of its position is usually cut back by frost each winter. However, each spring it comes again, rejuvenated. The delightful perfume of the crushed leaves often causes visitors to be amazed when they brush by the plant on a warm day when it will release its fragrance.

Magnolias

To have the maximum joy and pleasure from magnolias it is essential to take care in siting and cultivation. Although magnolia is classified as a shrub some species grow into sizeable trees. I am pleased that I planted several in the early years of the garden and so placed them that they have grown up protected and unharmed by the gales we have experienced from time to time. Like camellias they do appreciate our slightly acid soil and when their roots reached into the fractures of the old red sandstone underneath they simply took off.

We have four varieties. *Magnolia* × *soulangiana*, the best known magnolia, with its large white and purple-tinged flowers produced by the hundred, makes a sight in April admired by all privileged to see it. An even more beautiful plant flowering a week or so later is *M.* × *soulangiana* 'Alba Superba'—the flowers are very large, sweetly scented and from a distance appear to be made of white wax. *M. liliiflora* 'Nigra' produces its lovely dark purple flowers in May and often continues to flower well into June. Up to now it has been less generous with its growth and amount of flowers but every year there are two or three more blooms. Our earliest magnolia is *M. stellata*, the star magnolia, this is the easiest for a small garden because of its ultimate size. Here it flowers profusely in late March; when the frosts pass us by it is a terrific success and a great joy, announcing as it does the coming of spring.

We planted *Mahonia bealei* in a partially shaded position opposite the dining-room windows; it is not only a joy to look at but when the weather is mild the lily-of-the-valley scented flowers emit their perfume, pervading the surrounding area. Every Christmas without fail it is the centre piece in the flower arrangement on the dinner table. Its evergreen foliage is, of course, useful all the year through, especially when it gets its reddish glow. Apart for ground cover under trees I did regard *Mahonia aquifolium* almost as a weed and quite ungainly but Sheila Macqueen has reintroduced us to it, pointing out the beautiful colouring of the leaves, different in each season. In the spring the fragrance of its golden yellow flower spikes is an added bonus.

Another shrub we love for its perfume is the *Philadelphus*. We have two varieties in the garden. 'Belle Etoile' with single, white, chalice-shaped flowers flushed with pink at the base of fringed petals is one of the best for perfume. 'Virginal' is also strong scented and is possibly the best double variety, with enormous panicles of pure white flowers.

Potentillas

We regard a potentilla as a must for any garden, however small. It gives such a long display of its dainty flowers, right through the summer into the early autumn and no shrub is less fussy about its soil. We have three yellow varieties: 'Elizabeth', 'Katherine Dykes', and one of the newer ones 'Moonlight'. All of them are very generous with their buttercup yellow flowers. 'Red Ace' is the only non-yellow variety we have, the reddish colour of the flowers is best when the weather is dull; for greatest depth of flower colour plant this variety, and 'Tangerine', in semi-shade positions.

As we wanted in the early days to erect a living screen to blot out the black boards of the old 16th century cart shed, now our garage, we could not have done better than using *Ribes sanguineum* 'Pulborough Scarlet', the flowering currant. It is one of the easiest and quickest-to-grow shrubs. We have two wonderful plants—the growth is erect and strong and we contain it to the size we want it to be by pruning after it has flowered in April/May.

Senecio 'Sunshine' grows in several places in our garden; we grow it for its soft, grey foliage which stays on all through the winter. Its yellow, daisy-like flowers in July/August contribute little to its value as a worthwhile plant. Cutting off small branches and twigs frequently, for flower arrangements, helps to keep it in good shape. A cheerful yellow shrub for semi-shade is *Spartium junceum*, the Spanish broom; it makes a great show when in full bloom and has a sweet scent but it is a very untidy plant unless pruned regularly.

One of my special favourites comes into bloom by the end of April/beginning of May, *Spiraea* × *arguta* (bridal wreath). Every spring its arching branches carry festoons of dainty white flowers; we prune it carefully after flowering so that it makes new wood for flowering the following season.

A tree-like evergreen shrub we have used amongst the backcloth of trees is *Stranvaesia davidiana*. The sprays of hawthorn-like flowers in June are not very significant but the scarlet berries that follow add colour to the garden until after Christmas. The foliage also takes on reddish-brown hues which adds to the overall effect. It is subject to occasional die back and we cut out any branch that shows early signs of bacterial infection.

Syringas

The syringas (lilacs) are one of the few shrubs which are so beautiful in full flower but equally dull for the rest of the year. However, Clack's Farm without 'Charles Joly' with its dark purple to red flowers, 'Souvenir de Louis/Späth' with its deep wine-red, fully-scented trusses, 'Mrs. Edward Harding' with its double or almost double, scented red flowers and 'Madame Lemoine' with its panicles of wonderful white blossom, which was introduced before the turn of the century, would be unthinkable. They need about four years to settle down after transplanting but after that period one can enjoy them to the full each season. One or two old trees we inherited we have managed to rejuvenate by very drastic pruning during the winter. The Canadian hybrid lilacs settle down much quicker than the *Syringa vulgaris* types; *S. × josiflexa* 'Bellicent' with its fragrant rose coloured flowers is our favourite. We found a place for the species *S. microphylla* 'Superba', the small-leaved lilac. It covers itself with rose-pink flowers in late May/early June and again in September, and the fragrance is absolutely out of this world. The syringa species are probably the most suitable for the small garden. At Clack's Farm 'Superba' has lived within its limits 150 × 90 cm (5 × 3 ft) and is about 10 years old.

A truly superb group of shrubs for the smaller as well as the larger garden of any soil are the viburnums; all they ask for is good drainage. Our season starts in December with *Viburnum × bodnantense* in bloom; its deep pink flower buds open to fragrant, rose-coloured, tubular flowers in small clusters and it goes on producing its blossom throughout the winter. A frosty spell may brown some but when the frost is over, back comes the colour of fresh flowers—another must in our Christmas flower arrangements. A close second is *V. tinus* (laurustinus); planted near our front door, from Christmas until May it is covered first in pink buds and then by the fully opened heads of small white flowers offset by the dark green foliage. Without doubt the most spectacular of them all is *V. plicatum* (*V. tomentosum*) 'Lanarth'. This plant has few equals when in full flower, its 'shelves' filled to the brim with large clusters of snowy white flowers is natural beauty at its best, a pleasure we await every Maytime. It would be wrong to omit *V. carlesii*, another May-flowering variety with superbly scented heads of pink buds which open to white flowers, or *V. opulus* 'Sterile' the snowball tree with its yellow-green flowers, which later develop into white snowballs.

The end of our shrub alphabet brings us to the weigelas; they thrive anywhere providing they are fed. Our best loved ones are 'Newport Red' with its bright red flowers, 'Bristol Ruby' with ruby-red flowers, and the slower growing *Weigela florida* 'Variegata', which is always beautiful with its golden, variegated foliage, but never more so than when the rose-pink flowers on it are in full bloom. Of course many worthwhile garden shrubs have been omitted from the list but I did say at the beginning that the shrubs in Clack's Farm garden were our choice and I have not attempted to make a catalogue, only comments on our favourites.

CHAPTER TEN

FLOWERS AT CLACK'S FARM

When asked to do a BBC Woman's Hour radio programme on my favourite flower I had no hesitation—I did a piece on pansies. Apart from the fact that I started gardening with a packet of pansy seed in my tiny hot hands, their cheerful faces always bring joy to my heart. The only way to be sure that pansies succeed year after year is to move the site for growing them around the garden, to spray them regularly against greenfly and to deal with the slug problem. To keep pansies flowering all through the summer we cut all the flowers and seed heads off at least once a month, although it means no flowers for four or five days the plants repay us by being even more abundant than before.

Anchusa italica 'Royal Blue' grown from seed and flowering the following year, always finds a place in the garden. Grown in groups of five or more plants, the show of gentian blue heads three to four feet tall in June, is a glorious sight but they do need some support otherwise the first whisper of strong wind will blow them flat to the ground.

We would miss the colourful clumps of anemones in the spring and early summer, their cheerful blooms in a wide range of bright colours appear when the spring flowers are over and the summer colours have not yet arrived. We have never grown anemones from seed, preferring to start with the dry small corms which are so freely available. We particularly like the 'St Piran' strain with its long stems which make the flowers so suitable for cutting; left on the plants they last for several weeks.

Aquilegia (columbine)—although I like the old fashioned original flowers it is the long spurred hybrids that appeal especially to me. From seed sown in March we have plants flowering the following summer, when the blooms in their most delicate colours look like fairies dancing in the sunlight. I like them best planted in small groups against a darker background of a hedge, which not only shows up the colours to advantage but also gives them some protection against wind damage.

For late summer and early autumn colour we regularly grow asters but only the low-growing varieties, the ones that don't need staking. Ours are grown from seed and planted out in May. We always make sure that our asters are never planted in the same place two seasons in succession. We find asters very prone to attack by aphis and invariably ours need a couple of insecticidal sprays early in the season.

Aubrieta I know is classified as a common plant; it is found in most untidy gardens but who can deny that it gives so much for so little care. Our plants are renewed from time to time, replacements are grown from seed and allowed to flower before being planted out into their permanent positions. This allows us to be selective as regards colours; it is so easy to get an all blue/mauve collection to the exclusion of some of the more exciting pastel shades ranging from pink to the more positive colours such as red.

Begonias

Begonias of course are an all the year round joy, we make full use of the fibrous rooted varieties for bedding and from them I would pick 'Danica Red' and 'Salina' as my favourites. However, the recently introduced tuberous-rooted 'Non-stop' begonias won my affection in 1979 when, in a dreadful summer, groups planted in the open border provided displays of quality blooms that would have been a credit in any heated greenhouse. The colour range already includes yellow, rose, carmine, copper and orange. We not only use them for bedding but also pot them up for use as houseplants. The flowers are double, of good size and the colours are clear. We bring a range of the fibrous-rooted begonias from the borders into the house before the first autumn frost and then, soon after cutting them back, we have a superb display of flowers together with lovely foliage all through the winter. We adore varieties like 'Lloydii', ideal for hanging baskets but from November till March there is nothing to beat 'Lorraine Love Me' in a free standing set of cluster pots. The masses of pink flowers never fail to bring memories of sunshine and brighten the darkest winter's day.

In July and sometimes into August we adore two lovely clumps of *Campanula persicifolia*; they always do well in spite of being in partial shade. They are trouble free and never fail to give us a great display of erect stems covered with blue flowers, a flower arranger's delight as they last well in water. Once every three or four years we divide the plants and so go on increasing our plant stock and at the same time giving some of our gardening friends the opportunity to share our pleasure in growing them.

Before coming to Clack's Farm I used to grow indoor carnations at the Lenton Research Station but since living here time has not allowed me to give them the attention they need. But now with the co-operation of the British Carnation Society we have a space in a long border for some superb hardy carnations and border pinks. One border carnation we have grown from seed and also propagated from cuttings is 'Crimson Knight'. It is really terrific whether planted outside or grown as a pot plant. Its colour is a dark red and its perfume has to be experienced to be believed, a fragrance akin to that of the old fashioned clove pinks.

I certainly could not leave out chrysanthemums, although 'Arthur Billitt' and 'Gladys Billitt' are still grown, they have largely been superseded by early flowering spray varieties grown from cuttings. I still find it a real joy to care for chrysanthemums and sometimes I feel that I would like to go back to growing a November or December crop of really superb late flowering blooms, but time and greenhouse heating costs do not permit it.

Dahlias
It is difficult to know how to write in a few words sufficient praise of dahlias. If well cared for, there are no flowering plants more conducive to either a brilliantly colourful show in the garden or to a lovely arrangement indoors. We grow dahlias several ways, from tubers which are planted out in late spring or, for the more rewarding approach for getting really superb plants, we pot the tubers up in March in 25 cm (10 in) pots and propagate new plants from the young shoots. These plants give us better quality flowers than those grown from old tubers but it is necessary to have some heat for propagation and facilities for hardening off the young plants before they are planted out towards the end of May or early June. We do grow varieties from seed which we find are ideal for bedding out; they are a real asset giving us colour from late July until the end of October—in fact they go on flowering until the autumn frosts arrive.

A chance meeting with Colin Edwards of the Delphinium Society brought his favourite flower to our attention. His enthusiasm was contagious and led to planting some named varieties in a plot for BBC 2 'Gardeners' World'. The beauty and the majesty of the spikes during that first season left us with no alternative than to continue; now we have a much larger area devoted to these monarchs and they are also found in other parts of the garden. Contrary to general belief they are not difficult to grow since they grow well from seed and cuttings are fairly easy to strike. Their height can, of course, be a problem but some recently introduced metal link stakes which lock together around the plants give them the protection they need against wind damage. It only remains necessary to feed the plants and to make sure that slugs are dealt with before the winter, otherwise they feed on the underground buds which could even result in the death of the plant.

The perfume of cottage pinks (*Dianthus*) is another boyhood memory and I still love to plant the variety 'Mrs. Sinkins', an old-fashioned double white flower loaded with fragrance. Modern border dianthus are of course far superior in form and the collection planted in 1980 has given us a lot of pleasure but in many cases fragrance has been sacrificed for beauty. When a few years ago we grew 'Queen of Hearts' from seed we immediately fell in love with it, its masses of single scarlet blooms

BBC cameraman Jack Rooke 'shooting' the author on a daffodil session for BBC 2 'Gardeners' World'. Note the cable attached to the camera (an EMI 2001), which feeds the pictures to the scanner (p. 76), where they are processed further (April 1980).

were an unbelievable sight all through the summer. Now it always finds a place in the annual border. 'Queens Court' and 'Magic Charms' with their mixtures of colour came later but our favourite is still 'Queen of Hearts'.

Geraniums

I have always associated geraniums with a memory of an old friendly gardener in a green apron taking cuttings in August—the smell of his potting shed is something I shall never forget. But now with the progress in the development of geranium varieties from seed, we only take cuttings from a few of our special houseplant and hanging-basket varieties of which seed is not yet available. All our geraniums for bedding out are now grown from seed sown in January, most are F_1 hybrids and start to flower outside late June or early July. 'Sprinter' was one of the first F_1 hybrids but has now been surpassed by many more recent introductions which are more compact in growth habit. One of them I particularly like is 'Sonnet' with its clear pink blooms, other new outstanding varieties from the same breeder are 'Minuet', 'Caprice', 'Cadenza' and 'Rhapsody'; together they complete the full geranium colour range. 'Playboy', a dwarf and very compact variety with a considerable mixture of colours, is used freely at Clack's Farm for bedding simply because it does stand up to bad weather conditions during the summer.

We love gladioli, the tall flowering spikes always look so majestic when growing towards the back of the border. We plant the corms out each spring, the taller the variety the deeper we plant them so that staking can be kept to a minimum. In the autumn we lift the corms and gather up the cormlets (offset corms) as well, for drying off as quickly as possible near the central heating boiler. Gladioli need a rich, well-drained soil to do justice to their potential. We always give ours an organic fertilizer worked into the soil at planting time.

Flower arrangers go into raptures over hellebores and so do we. They are a great asset to any garden, especially here where we have a number of shady corners. We have many species and the flowering starts in December with *Helleborus niger*, the Christmas rose, very soon after that *H. corsicus* starts to produce its huge clusters of pale green, cup-shaped, pendent blooms. They last so long that often we can still pick some flower heads in June; left to seed we have the pleasure of supplying our friends with small seedlings found around the mother plants. Also during the late winter we have *Helleborus foetidus* flowering behind the alpine garden; again they seed freely and every year we collect a trayful of seedlings for distribution. The many *orientalis* species with their handsome foliage and upright carried, bowl-shaped flowers do very well here. Again they thrive in the shade.

Impatiens sultanii, the busy Lizzie, is certainly one of our favourite house plants. Feed them and, if need be, spray them for greenfly and they go on looking healthy and flower for months on end. Although it is mainly a houseplant not many people realise that it is a very worthwhile subject for bedding out—planted outside early in June they quickly make large plants and flower until the first autumn frost. If amongst the plants we find an outstanding specimen we lift it in late summer and propagate it from cuttings, a very easy operation.

The front of Clack's Farm house would be bare in the summer without the so aptly named morning glory (*Ipomea*) 'Heavenly Blue' climbing up strings to the gutters. Each morning a fresh batch of Mediterranean sky-blue flowers are there to greet us. The height to which the plants ultimately reach is a clear indication of the season's weather. In 1975 and 1976 they passed the bedroom windows and were still flowering near the guttering when the first frost came, but in 1979 they were struggling about 2 metres (6½ft) up when an August gale broke the strings and put an end to them. It was a lesson; we now use a combination of nylon and fillis string to prevent a repeat of the disaster.

The author among dahlias grown from rooted cuttings, supplied by the National Dahlia Society. Note the peaches and apricots growing against the fences in the background (September 1974).

When in the spring of 1980 we had a few spare plants, we decided to grow them on in the greenhouse and eventually they twined themselves around the uprights. From the middle of July onwards it was a sight to behold, the flowers being nearly twice their normal size and absolutely perfect in shape and colour.

Lilies

No plants are happier in Clack's Farm soil than lilies, they multiply freely and, if allowed, will seed themselves to such an extent that on occasions they have almost become a weed, justifying the saying that a weed is only a plant in the wrong place. All our plants of *L. regale* have been grown from seed, from start to finish they take about four years to get into their full flowering strides to provide an annual show of great beauty but they must be left undisturbed. The madonna lily (*Lilium candidum*) is I think one of the most beautiful of all lilies and certainly the richest as regards perfume. Some years ago I was given the opportunity to lift a few bulbs from a garden in Woodborough, Nottinghamshire; the dear old lady was tired of them and she did not appreciate the brown, half-dead looking stems at flowering time. I lifted the bulbs one Friday evening and planted them the following morning at Clack's

The beginning of a new and happy partnership at Clack's Farm, Arthur and Riet Billitt on their wedding day, 28 May 1977.

Farm, where with their noses close to the surface and their roots subsequently down in some well-rotted compost. They have never looked back. Every July they load the air with fragrance; we don't mind if the stems do die down quickly afterwards—that is just their natural behaviour.

From a limited and careful start with lilies we have now got a collection of new varieties from the Rosewarne Experimental Station, several with well known Cornish names, e.g. 'St. Blazey', 'St Day', 'Falmouth'. Most of these have colours which range from a deep mahogany to shades of orange; they too flower in June or even July. We have recently added more lilies to our collection; one of them, 'Enchantment', has been flowering freely during the last two years and is now a joy to behold each July.

I still have a passion for lupins but alas the results of good work done by the late George Russell in his Yorkshire garden have largely disappeared. Now we still grow the so-called Russell strain, they are beautiful, but not a patch on George's original collection of bi-coloured flowers.

Our garden would not be the same in the summer without marigolds, even in the poorest summer when many annuals fail they are there and go on until the first autumn frost. Our favourite must be a fairly new one 'Nell Gwynn', aptly named as its wide open flowers reminds one of oranges and lemons.

We are lucky in having a small part of the garden damp enough for growing the lovely blue Himalayan poppies, *Meconopsis betonicifolia* (*M. baileyi*). We started with just a couple of plants; now, by saving our own seed, we maintain a regular supply of new seedlings. The fresh seed germinates quickly—we keep the seedlings in a cold greenhouse or frame during the winter and plant them out in May. If by any chance they produce a flower stem in the first year we remove it; this allows the plants to establish themselves in preparation for flowering the following season.

Two other annual flowering plants we could not do without are the petunias and sweet peas, we find that the recently introduced petunias are now so good that they are a must for bedding out; they stand up to bad weather and go on flowering well into September. Sweet peas are a great joy, not only for their many colours but above all for their fragrance—the pleasure of being able to pick masses of flowers at one time and two days later being able to gather another armful! There is simply no flower to beat sweet peas for colour, perfume and generosity, and they make flower arranging an easy task.

Roses

In common with most gardeners roses must be near the top of my list of favourite flowers, the climate of this country suits them so well that no garden would be complete without them. Right from the time when the wilderness we inherited began to be transformed into a garden, roses have been a feature of Clack's Farm garden. The rose beds in the ornamental garden are a mixture of floribundas and hybrid teas. On the front of the house two 'Pink Perpetue' climbing roses excel themselves, other climbers are to be found in the Royal National Rose Society's plot, which is featured from time to time in 'Gardener's World'. In 1981 we decided that, after 25 years, the rose beds in the ornamental garden should be given a rest. We cleared out all the bushes, this providing the opportunity to increase the depth of the shrub border at the back, before seeding the area. We are more than pleased with the result as it gives the whole garden a more spacious look.

Of course we grow many more annual flowers such as *Mesembryanthemum*, *Nicotiana*, larkspur and many more—they all contribute to make Clack's Farm garden a riot of colour. We would not be without our primulas, polyanthus or primroses; we love all our plants but there are too many to name individually.

Each spring we enjoy the galaxy of spring flowers grown from bulbs, early in February the first aconites and snowdrops appear to greet us and herald the beginning of a new season, a little later the much larger snowdrop 'Mr. S. Arnot' opens, then come the crocus species with their dainty flowers followed by the larger cultivated ones. We have many varieties of daffodils and narcissi, some unnamed seedlings amongst them. We do love them particularly when they stand up firmly to cold wintry weather without coming to any harm. After the great show of colour we are left with the foliage, but we leave it to die down naturally and then, before the autumn, we apply some fish, blood and bone fertilizer to the area, thus ensuring that we get a good display the following spring. We do grow some tulips; we prefer the smaller-flowered, early spring-flowering species which can be left in the ground year after year without degenerating.

AFTER THOUGHTS

Whilst now in 1981 we can look back over a quarter of a century's endeavour and be somewhat satisfied with the results, if it were possible to start all over again we would not repeat our mistakes. However much experience one has in gardening, not everything goes according to plan—there are some things we would not do again and we failed to do others, matters for regret perhaps, but we cannot go back in time and have to be content. Making a new garden takes years and whilst twenty-five years may be a brief span in the life of many trees, it is more than a third of the average gardener's lifetime. In 1956, the year we started to alter Clack's Farm from its derelict condition to what it has become, was just eleven years prior to my retirement—at every stage I felt the pressures of urgency, there was no time to waste. Making a garden without the employment of labour meant that at every stage it was our garden, but at all times due consideration had to be given to the size of the task. Could we with the help of Bert do the jobs at the right time and do them in the best possible way? Having many friends in the horticultural world was an enormous asset; they took a great interest in our efforts, involving as it did a 160 mile drive every week-end.

One of the main things I regret is not having been more selective in choosing the rhododendrons and azaleas, I accepted a job lot instead of carefully selecting the right varieties which by now would have grown into a collection to be proud of. Instead, at this late stage, we are now seriously thinking of re-arranging that area in the garden and probably replanting without including rhododendrons which are so dull out of their flowering season. Instead of planting a *Wisteria sinensis* by the corner of the house just to cover a downpipe, we should have got down to the task of immediately fixing training wires along the whole length of the south-facing front wall. What a magnificent sight that would have been by now, when in June the wisteria is in flower. Instead, it still clings to the downpipe and flowers in a corner difficult to see. The only compensation for having the flowering cherry 'Accolade' in front of the house is that the bullfinches warn us that it is time to cover the fruit trees and to check the fruit cages; even the much maligned 'Kanzan' would have been a better choice. Amongst our earliest planting failures was *Magnolia grandiflora* 'Exmouth'. After five years it died for some unknown reason. I should have planted another one immediately, but as it can take 20 years before it decides to flower I did not think it was worthwhile—how we regret it now.

The bright idea of covering some of the farm buildings with hederas (ivies) was fine until both the walls and the roofs were covered with a mass of growth at least 30 cm (1 ft) thick. The sparrows and garden warblers loved the cover but in time it became necessary to remove the ivy to save the tiled roofs of the pigsties. Alas, we lost the garden warblers, they were great friends, but we were not sorry to deprive the sparrows of their habitat as they had become a real nuisance in the garden. The removal of the bird table together with the elimination of the ivy brought about a dramatic change. Whereas before our forsythias, crown imperials, polyanthus and primroses had been attacked on a grand scale each spring, now we were able to enjoy them to the full without resorting to cottoning, netting or spraying.

As mentioned in the chapter on tree fruits we had to give up growing peaches, etc. out in the open, under glass is our only hope of real success. If we could start again all our apples would be on M 9 rootstock, to save me fighting the trees each year with a pair of secateurs to contain them to the size I want them to grow, as either cordons or dwarf bush trees.

Had we known that greenhouse heating costs were going to rise to such heights, we would certainly have arranged the garden so that the greenhouses would have been near enough to the house to be connected up to our solid fuel central heating system. As it is we have virtually abandoned electrical heating in the greenhouses and switched over to paraffin heating with double banks of 3 m- (10 ft-) water pipes, efficient, safe and not too extravagant. Three years ago we installed an underground water distribution system with points for hose and sprinkler connections in strategic positions; a late decision but it is a great boon and very efficient. However, when the plastic pipes were laid the trenches were not dug deep enough with the result that when I am digging I can in an absent-minded moment be confronted with too much water close at hand, so next winter we intend to remedy the fault and re-lay all the pipes well below the depth of a spade or fork.

The thought of those farmyard antiques buried deep below the soil in the old cattle yard, now the visitors tea garden, still troubles me on